The City of Influence

A BUSINESS TALE

influenceinternational

To all the official and unofficial editors inside our cities of influence whose feedback contributed so greatly to the writing and publishing of this book.

Laura College	George Stewart	Kaisa Crossley
Lynna Stewart	JoAnna Stewart	Alan Wilson
Jeff Rust	Joni Wright	Brandon Jeppson
Laura Corbridge	Julie Andersen	Brent Bingham
Kelsey Harris	May Benson	Naoma Wilkinson
Brent Crane	Abigail Stewart	Jacob Hoehne
Angela Eschler	Jeff Reeves	Marcie Hill
Debbie Harrison	John Curtis	Kelsie Rose
Delys Snyder	Chris Shurian	Maren Turnidge
Valerie Holladay	Tyler O'Steen	Chris Dexter
Melanie Ballard	Jacque Brown	Steven Roy
Richard Tripp	Deann Huish	Dan Capel
Annette Lyon	Trent Sutton	Rick Ables
Josh Rowley	Richard Swan	Melinda Logan
Mark Romney	Deborah Swan	Ron Nielsen
Kristen Knight	Margie Call	Cory Mahaffey
Jane Ann Craig	James Mayfield	Lance Black
Don Boyle	Don Chiniquy	Bill Brady
Cameron Packer	Kip Enger	Richard Roberts

TABLE OF CONTENTS

1.

Jack Green

You never miss the water until the well has run dry.

—Irish Proverb

Jack sat up gasping for air. His sweat-soaked shirt was clinging to his skin, and the rapid pounding of his heart echoed loudly in his ears.

It was just a dream, he told himself as he recognized the familiar shapes in his darkened bedroom. He looked over the shoulder of his sleeping wife at the clock sitting on her nightstand. The glowing numbers read 12:07 a.m.

Rolling over, he tried to force himself back to sleep, but it was no use. He finally pushed back the blanket and made his way down the stairs.

As he walked through the quiet house, the violent images of his nightmare began replaying through his mind. His family had always teased him about being a hypochondriac, but this time he was certain something was really wrong. For three straight months he'd been alternating between insomnia and night terrors, and it was getting worse.

As Jack walked down the hall he saw the lamp in his office was still on. He'd been spending so much time away from his family that he'd recently added the office to his home. Sitting at his desk, Jack moved aside a tray stacked high with financial reports and legal documents and switched on his computer. When he opened his inbox, his heart sank: twenty-nine new e-mails. Although he'd just finished a book on positive thinking, he was willing to bet that none of them contained good news.

As he scanned through the subject lines, he spotted his teenage nick-name "Green Machine" and opened it. The message was from an old friend asking when they could get together for lunch. Jack realized that it had been almost six months since he'd seen Mark. They'd been inseparable in high school, but Jack couldn't seem to find time for anyone these days.

He closed the e-mail and noticed another one flagged as urgent. The subject line read "Tomorrow's Battle." With a puzzled frown, Jack opened the message and read its contents:

```
Gladiator,

Only by the intervention of the gods do you live to see
another dawn. Your cowardly performance on the field of
battle continues to provide little drama for my crowds,
but as long as your heart still beats inside your chest, I
am obligated to schedule your next match.

Please arrive early.


Sincerely,
Victor Sludge
Director of Coliseum Events
```

As Jack stared at the monitor, his mouth dropped open in disbelief. Was it possible his nightmares had found a way to torment his waking hours as well? Suddenly the screen snapped shut, replaced by an error notification. Jack reopened his mailbox and searched through the messages, but the e-mail had disappeared.

Maybe my brain is still asleep, he thought, trying to push down the panic rising in his chest. In an effort to distract his mind Jack began organizing his desk. He gathered stray pens and highlighters and put them back in the cup beside the computer. He then began separating the overdue bills from his banking statements and tax returns. Underneath the clutter, he uncovered a packet of information and read the large yellow sticky attached to it:

Jack,

Here are the financial reports I promised. Sorry, but it looks like we're going to be short again this week. I'll put the other payments on hold, but if we're going to make payroll, I'll need an additional thirty thousand by Friday.

Dan

In a small fit of rage, Jack jerked open the middle drawer and swept the papers in.

Out of sight, out of mind.

He was about to slam the drawer shut, when he spotted the corner of a leather-bound book peeking out from underneath the stack of papers.

That's where you went. I've been looking for you.

The book was the early journal of Patrick O'Flannery, the business partner of Jack's great-great grandfather George Green. Despite impossible odds, George and Patrick had become two of New York's most influential industrialists, and their rags-to-riches story had always fascinated Jack.

The only thing known about George's early life was that he'd left the family farm for New York City when he was about fifteen years old. Even less had been known about Patrick's background—until now. The brittle paper and smudged ink of the recently discovered journal provided a detailed account of how Patrick and his family had narrowly escaped starvation during the Irish Potato Famine by joining the throng of immigrants that had flooded into the United States during the 1840s.

Jack devoured the journal's contents in just a few sittings, but to his frustration, the account ended with Patrick's arrival in America. It didn't cover the period of time when Patrick had met George or give any clues about how they had been able to achieve their legendary success.

What would they do in my place? he asked himself as he absently leafed through the journal's yellowing pages, his thoughts going back to the subject that occupied almost all his waking hours—his struggling business. It didn't seem possible it had only been four years since he'd decided to start his own company; it felt more like twenty.

I've completely ruined my life. What was I thinking?

In Jack's mind, the story began replaying from the beginning. It all started the day Jack invited his friend Monty James to lunch. During the course of their conversation, they discovered they had both always dreamed of starting their own businesses. By the end of their fifth sushi roll, they had the beginnings of a business plan. Using their middle names, they had called the company Dillon-Parker Design and felt certain they were about to revolutionize the world of brand management. Because of his background and business experience, Jack was given the role of president; it would be his job to lead the company to success.

I walked out of there on cloud nine, Jack remembered.

Images of Dillon-Parker's grand opening flashed through Jack's mind. He vividly remembered the entire staff surrounding him as he cut the ribbon, raising their glasses to toast the arrival of the world's greatest force in advertising.

But the dream had been short-lived. Dillon-Parker had launched their business at the height of a boom market, and while the first twelve months had been nirvana, the second twelve were slow torture. Eight of their top ten clients had either gone out of business or decided to significantly reduce the amount of money they were spending on their brand. For the last two years, the company had managed to survive, but Jack knew his time was running out. Even his best estimates put him out of business within six months.

The past year had been the worst of Jack's life. It had taken him only ten months to burn through his entire two-million-dollar line of credit. After that was gone, Jack had begun liquidating his personal assets: first his real estate investments, then his stocks, and finally, just yesterday, he had taken every penny of equity out of their home.

His dream had officially turned into a nightmare.

It should be working! What am I leaving out? Jack slammed the palm of his hand on the desk, oblivious to the resultant sting. "Will someone please tell me what I'm missing?" he asked aloud.

Half expecting an answer, he sat in silence for a few minutes. Then, with a sigh, he tucked the journal under his arm and headed for the kitchen. Lately, eating seemed to be the only thing that eased his pain.

He opened the refrigerator door and rummaged around, finally emerging with a few red-chili burritos and a quart of chocolate peanut-butter ice cream. While waiting for the burritos to heat up, he took out a mixing bowl and started scooping ice cream into it. As he moved around the kitchen, he found it painful to look at the marble countertops and steel appliances. He and his wife had purchased their new home with the assumption of prosperity; he'd never even contemplated the possibility of failure. When he thought of the current state of his business—and the prospect of losing everything he'd worked so hard for—a knot tightened in the pit of his stomach and he found it difficult to breathe.

Mercifully, the microwave buzzer interrupted his thoughts, and Jack began loading up his arms with food. Going into the den, he settled himself into his favorite chair. As Jack set the bowl of ice cream on a side table, he saw his daughter's picture book and felt a stab of guilt. He'd arrived home that evening to discover her asleep on his chair with the book clutched in her tiny hands. His wife had explained that she'd insisted on waiting up for the bedtime story he'd promised to read her. The brightly illustrated pigs on the cover were a painful reminder that Jack was failing in much more than just his business.

As he settled back in his chair, Dillon-Parker's story resumed playing in his mind. He remembered the exhilaration he'd experienced as he pinpointed the perfect spot to build their new offices. His good friend, Murray Matthews, pulled a few strings at Oak Grove Community Bank to secure his line of credit as well as the money for the real estate. Jack also convinced six of his colleagues to leave their current jobs to join his new management team. But his biggest accomplishment had been selling his security-loving wife on the idea. He'd been on fire, completely unstoppable.

Now, four years later, the company was still losing money every month. Jack had tried to trim costs wherever he could, but it seemed like every other week he was scrambling to make payroll. To make matters worse, just before he had left the office that day he'd received a call from an attorney informing him that a major client had just declared bankruptcy and didn't plan on paying their $75,000 invoice. Despite his best efforts, the company was now spinning out of control.

In a desperate attempt to distract his mind, Jack reached for the remote. In the past he'd avoided television, feeling his time was better spent working toward his goals.

And look where that's gotten me.

2.

Patrick O'Flannery

It is difficult to put a wise head on young shoulders.

—Irish Proverb

As Jack flipped through the channels, he came across a black-and-white film version of *A Christmas Carol*. It seemed an odd programming choice for mid-September, but he figured it was better than an infomercial and settled back to watch.

Jacob Marley had just appeared to warn Scrooge of the fate that awaited him as a consequence of his miserly ways, his clanking chains providing a chilling visual aid for his words. The eeriness of the scene brought Jack's nightmares back to the forefront of his mind, but he felt compelled to continue watching.

On the screen, a terrified Scrooge protested, "But you were always a good man of business, Jacob."

"Business!" cried the ghost. "Mankind was my business. The common welfare was my business. The dealings of my trade were but a drop of water in the comprehensive ocean of my business."

A sense of impending doom swept through Jack, but he found it impossible to take his eyes from the screen.

Jacob Marley seemed to be speaking directly to him, "I am here tonight to warn you that you have a chance of escaping my fate. You will be haunted by spirits tonight, and without their visits you cannot hope to shun the path I tread."

The stillness of the room seemed to intensify—as if every object in it was poised and waiting for something to happen.

Suddenly a hearty voice from behind Jack called out, "Good evening, lad!"

Jack leapt from his chair and turned to face the intruder. To his amazement he saw a man sitting on his leather couch eating popcorn from a large plastic bowl. Wisps of red hair peeked out from underneath his cap and a bag of golf clubs lay at his feet, the bag's exterior embroidered with a shamrock insignia.

Speaking with a thick Irish accent, the man continued, "You'll be excusing my not doing my own introduction, but 'tis terrible difficult to compete with Jacob Marley. Since he retired, the Foundation's had quite a time finding an adequate replacement. But enough of that! We'd best be getting started."

The man reached into his golf bag and pulled out a small laptop.

"What?" Jack finally choked out.

"I've been assigned as your trainer," the man explained pleasantly, as though they were old friends sitting down to lunch. "Your call came in at . . ." He flipped open a laptop, his fingers moving like lightning across the keys. "12:29 a.m." He checked his watch with a furrowed brow. "We have a ten-minute guaranteed arrival time, and I'm a wee bit late. But I'm hoping you'll be kind enough to overlook that, seeing as how the call was made outside normal business hours."

"There must be some mistake," Jack mumbled, rubbing his eyes.

"No mistake. The fee was electronically charged to your credit card." The stranger's fingers raced over the keys again. "The number was 9876 … saints above!" the man exclaimed in sudden comprehension. "A Foundation account."

Seeing the bewildered look on Jack's face, the man quickly explained, "Forgive me, lad. I was in such a state just getting here that I only glanced over your file. Let's see if I can explain." He rubbed his chin reflectively. "You see, the foundation I work for sometimes takes special cases pro bono when they feel the need is great and the potential high. You must've qualified on both counts."

The man stopped and leaned forward slightly, examining Jack with a puzzled expression. "Have you and I met? Because you do be putting me in mind of someone."

He pulled out a manila folder from the golf bag, and Jack could see a sheaf of papers with his photograph clipped to the top. The man scanned through the pages, then suddenly his head snapped up and he stared at Jack in astonishment.

"Glory be! 'Tis a wonder I didn't be seeing the family resemblance right off." He had a twinkle in his eye as he stretched out his hand to shake Jack's. "I don't believe we've been properly introduced. Patrick O'Flannery at your service."

Jack automatically reached out to shake Patrick's hand, though he half expected his flesh to slide right through that of the other man's.

"Oh, I get it," Jack said, feeling a wave of relief flood through him. "I'm still dreaming!"

"A common response," Patrick replied, nodding. "That's what Scrooge thought as well. He was another pro bono case, and although it was considered a bit of a risk at the time, the whole thing ended quite brilliantly. It's cited fourteen times in the handbook, you know."

Jack dug his fingernails into his palms, trying to create enough pain to wake himself up.

"What a grand joke sending me in without a warning word!" Patrick continued, slapping his palm against his knee. "But it's delighted I am to be here all the same. I owe a great debt to George Green, and one I'll never be able to fully repay, but it appears as if I'm to be given the chance to try."

"But you can't be Patrick O'Flannery! You died over a hundred years ago!" Jack finally exclaimed. It seemed pointless to argue with someone who didn't exist, but he couldn't help himself.

"Now then, I can't be explaining all the ins and outs of life and death. You'll just have to be trusting that I am who I say." Patrick stopped short as he caught sight of the journal on the table, "Ah! Now there's a sight that brings back memories."

Jack instinctively reached out and picked up the journal. "I've been reading it for the past couple of days. To tell you the truth, I haven't been able to put it down."

Patrick took the book from Jack, gently rubbing its cracked leather binding as he spoke. "Aye, you would be relating to this part of my story. You're in the middle of your own kind of famine, aren't you? That's why I'm here."

"Yeah, it looks like they pulled you out of a pretty important appointment," Jack said, observing Patrick's striped shirt and khakis with a trace of amusement.

"Now, Jack Green, that kind of thinking right there is the root of your problem," Patrick replied. "Why do you be supposing so many business students take golfing lessons? Do you have the least notion how much business takes place over a nine iron? Mergers, partnerships, securing big accounts—they've all been cemented over a wee ball and heaps of grass."

Then, as though he was imparting a great secret, Patrick said, "I'll risk a wager that you be one of those lads who think that business is all about numbers and transactions. But business is about *relationships.*"

Jack looked at him incredulously. "Let me get this straight. My great-great grandfather's business partner came back from the dead to tell me that the answer to my problems is playing more golf?"

Patrick threw his hands up in exasperation. "Do you be having some problems with your hearing, Jack Green?" he asked. "Because you don't seem to be listening. I didn't say business is about golf. I said business is about relationships."

A tinkling rendition of "Danny Boy" rang out and Jack jumped back as though he'd been bitten. The sound seemed to be originating from the golf bag at Patrick's feet.

"My apologies, lad!" Flustered, Patrick quickly dove into his golf bag and turned off the phone. "Turning off the cell phone is rule number one in the Code of Conduct."

Jack stood up and headed for the bathroom.

"Where are you off to? We'll be hard set to finish by morning as it is," Patrick called after him.

"To get some medication," Jack called over his shoulder. "I'm so sleep deprived I've gone delusional and am hallucinating a four-foot Irish Bobby Jones."

Patrick raised himself up to his full height and protested, "I'm well over five feet."

Jack ignored him. "Or maybe I've finally fallen asleep and you're my brain's twisted version of *It's a Wonderful Life.*"

"One of my favorite movies!" Patrick said, his eyes shining. When Jack didn't respond, Patrick called after him, "Heed this. I'm not a dream, and you shouldn't be so surprised, seeing as I'm here per your request."

"What request? I didn't ask you for anything," Jack called out as he unscrewed the lid of a small prescription bottle.

"Begging your pardon, but you did." Patrick typed furiously on his laptop. "At exactly 12:29 a.m. you said, 'Will someone please tell me what I'm missing?'"

Two pills slipped from Jack's grip and clattered onto the tile floor. He stepped out of the bathroom, his eyes wide with surprise.

Patrick continued, "But if you don't be wanting me services after all, I'll be going. I was in the middle of the game of my life, you know."

"Look," Jack finally said, "as nice as it is to meet you, I'm honestly at a point where I can't afford to waste any more energy on something that isn't going to work."

"Suffering ducks, lad, you could give a mule lessons in stubbornness!" Patrick exclaimed. "What other choice do you have? You've tried everything you could think of yourself and have come up all sixes and sevens.

So, I'll be asking you one more time, Jack Green, will you be wanting to know what you're missing or not?"

For the first time, Jack entertained the possibility that this might really be happening. He slowly ran his fingers through his hair, trying to forecast the possible consequences of accepting Patrick's offer.

"My life is coming apart at the seams. If things don't change soon, I'll lose everything," Jack admitted. He paused for a minute, then added reluctantly, "Yes, I want to know, but what do I have to do?"

"Well, first off, I'll be needing a little participation. Like the saying goes: 'Neither give cherries to pigs nor advice to a fool,'" Patrick said.

Jack sighed. "Well, like you said. I've got nothing to lose."

As he spoke these words, the grandfather clock in the hallway struck one o'clock. The gong was louder and longer than normal, and it increased in volume until it was deafening. Jack put his hands over his ears and squeezed his eyes shut.

3

The Gladiator

A man may be his own ruin.

—Irish Proverb

Jack felt the pressure of a dense crowd pushing up against him, and when he opened his eyes, he found himself surrounded by thousands of people. He didn't understand the language they spoke, but judging from the way they were dressed it appeared as though he'd somehow been transported to ancient Rome.

Desperately searching the crowd, he spotted Patrick and pushed toward him. As soon as he was close enough, Jack grabbed his arm.

"This is going too far, even for one of my psychotic dreams," he said through clenched teeth. "Where am I?"

Instead of answering Jack's question, Patrick held up two leather squares, each stamped with an intricate design.

"'Tis your lucky day, lad. I just happen to have two tickets for the Senators Pavillion," he said.

A blast of trumpets sounded, and the crowd began lumbering forward, the mass of bodies sweeping them toward the entrance of an enormous coliseum. They passed beneath two massive archways, and the interior of the coliseum came into view. Jack's jaw dropped in astonishment as he looked around and saw tens of thousands of people slowly filling the stone risers.

"We'd best be finding our seats," Patrick said nudging him forward.

Navigating a labyrinth of stone stairways, they eventually arrived inside an enclosed balcony overlooking the arena. Jack's eyes were immediately drawn to the bright silk awning that shielded a table full of appetizing dishes.

"I think you'll enjoy a bit of the shrimp and melons and even the fish soufflé," Patrick said as they picked up their plates. He then gestured to a dish near the end of the table and added, "But I'd steer clear of that one."

"Why?" Jack asked, leaning forward to examine the dish. "What is it?"

"Peacock tongues," Patrick replied, grinning at Jack's disgusted expression. "They're not bad with a pinch of cinnamon, but I don't think you'd fancy them."

They took their seats, and after successfully balancing his heaping plate on his lap, Jack looked out over the playing field for the first time. It was surrounded by formidable fifteen-foot walls, and large boulders and wooden structures dotted the field of play. As he examined the field, Jack was suddenly struck with an overpowering sense of déjà vu. The field was undeniably familiar, but identifying where he'd seen it before seemed just beyond his reach.

Then a wave of recognition broke over him, followed by a second wave of nausea.

"I can't stay here," he gasped, spilling his food on the stone floor as he rose to his feet.

"Steady there, lad," Patrick said, laying a hand on his arm. "Why don't you just take a breath and tell me what's wrong."

Cold fear began pulsing through Jack's veins. "You don't understand. I've fought a thousand battles on that field. That place is my nightmare!"

Patrick nodded. "Aye, I know all about your dreams lad. That's the reason I brought you here—to empty the box so we can fill it again."

Their conversation was interrupted by the sound of screeching metal against stone. Inside the arena two chains spun into motion, lifting an iron gate until it locked into place. The trumpets sounded again as a lone figure passed through the gate.

Watching in horrified fascination, Jack sank back in his seat. Although he'd never seen it from this perspective before, he remembered the dank smell of the tunnel from which the gladiator had just exited and could almost feel the weight of the armor on his chest and shoulders. The warrior he was looking at was himself.

The gladiator placed a helmet on his head, shifting it back and forth until it slipped into place. Then, after selecting a shield and sword from the stockpile of weapons, he climbed the raised platform at the center of the arena. With one fluid motion, he raised his sword high in the air; the crowd responded with a deafening roar.

Without warning, the doors on the east and west sides of the arena heaved open, and two armored chariots appeared, each driven by a gladiator. One of the gladiators, arrayed in blue and gray, skillfully guided his team of horses into the desired position. With the flick of his whip, the huge animals lunged forward and quickly gained in speed as they raced across the arena toward the lone gladiator.

"I can't do this again," Jack muttered under his breath.

"Better to watch him than to stand in his place," Patrick whispered back.

Jack looked at Patrick incredulously. "Is that supposed to make me feel better?"

Jack watched his gladiator-self dive out of the way, dust billowing around him as he fell to the ground. The other gladiator wheeled around his chariot and headed back. This time he struck a blow with his trident, ripping off Jack's breastplate and tearing cruelly into the flesh underneath. Back in the pavillion, Jack clutched his side, but his eyes never left the field.

Staggering toward a great stone monolith at the edge of the arena, Jack watched himself hide behind it as the other two gladiators engaged each other. Their battle was brief, and within minutes the same gladiator who had injured Jack raised his bloody sword in victory.

As the crowd chanted its approval, the victorious charioteer wheeled his horses around and drew out a large spear.

"He's going to kill me, isn't he?" Jack groaned, putting his hands over his eyes, but continuing to watch through his fingers.

As the chariot rumbled past, Jack's gladiator-self jumped up behind the charioteer and, using all his weight, dragged his opponent onto the ground. Taking a step backward, he unsheathed a dagger and plunged it into his opponent. The crowd let out a deafening cheer as the opposing gladiator slumped to the ground, and red and white rose petals filled the air, slowly fluttering to the arena floor.

Looking around at the chanting crowd, Jack finally blurted out, "What are they saying? After every battle they chant the same words."

"*Habet, hoc habet,*" Patrick explained. "It means 'He is finished.'"

Jack watched himself salute the crowd, then collapse. Two slaves came onto the field and carried him away, leaving a dark trail of blood behind them.

"Am I going to be all right?" Jack asked.

"Will you listen to that," Patrick said as the crowd continued to cheer wildly, seemingly unaware that Jack had asked a question. "The whole lot of them on their feet hailing you as a hero. This is quite the dream you've been having."

"It's not a dream—it's a nightmare. I've been coming here nearly every night for three weeks. Sometimes I win, but more often I . . ." Jack's voice trailed off. "Needless to say, I don't really look forward to going to sleep anymore."

4.

Choosing Sides

As the old cock crows the young cock learns.

—Irish Proverb

Without warning, the coliseum was swallowed up in blackness. Jack stood tensely in the darkness, ready to defend himself, but when the familiar chimes of the clock in his hallway began to play, he exhaled a sigh of relief; he was home again. He heard a click, and the room was suddenly illuminated. Turning around, he saw Patrick sitting in the leather armchair, the lamp softly bathing him in light.

"Well, lad, how'd you be liking the sport?"

"I think I'd rather have eaten the peacock tongues and skipped the main attraction," Jack replied as he sank into a chair facing Patrick. "Why is this happening? Why do I turn into a gladiator every night?"

"The gladiator is only a symbol, lad—a symbol for the way you're choosing to manage your business. Truth be told, you're living the life of a gladiator by day and by night. The only difference is in one arena you wear a breastplate and carry a sword while in the other you wear a business suit and hold a briefcase."

Patrick's gaze seemed to pierce through Jack as he spoke.

"A gladiator views the world through Darwin's eyes," Patrick continued. "It's survival of the fittest for these lads and lasses. They've been taught that only the strongest, fastest and most ruthless will survive. For gladiators, business is a jungle, and they believe they only have two choices: they can either become a predator or someone else's dinner. Would that be sounding about right?"

"A little melodramatic, but I guess it's true," Jack admitted reluctantly.

"What I'm trying to tell you, Jack Green, is that you're a business version of the ancient gladiators—and an average one at best," Patrick said. "And because of this your business will die on the field of battle and your gladiator friends will do nothing more than write off their losses and move along to the next contender."

As the full impact of Patrick's meaning hit, Jack felt his body stiffen and he was suddenly on his feet.

"Hold on. Are you trying to say this is my fault?" he demanded. "Without me this company wouldn't have had a snowball's chance in hell."

Jack started to pace, his voice rising in intensity. "I work an insane number of hours every week and have contributed every financial resource I have, not to mention my physical and emotional health. If this business has any success it's due to my efforts, and if it fails it's because no one else has the same level of commitment!"

Jack slammed himself back into his seat, glaring at Patrick.

Patrick knelt beside him and spoke quietly. "Aye. You've fought match after match and you've the battle scars to prove it. You've worked harder, fought smarter, and sacrificed more than anyone else." Patrick gently laid a hand on Jack's arm. "I'm not saying you haven't done everything you can, lad. What I'm saying is, it's just not enough."

"Oh, it's comforting to know that *everything* isn't enough," Jack retorted.

"Perhaps the time has come for me to be sharing a bit more about my life back in Ireland," Patrick said, returning to the seat across from Jack. "'Tis not a time I care to be remembering, but it may help you to hear it."

Jack tried to hold on to his anger, but he felt it draining away as Patrick told his story. His words, lilting with the accent of his native country, captivated Jack as completely as the journal had.

Lightly touching on how he had met his wife, Molly, and on the happy arrival of their two sons, Patrick moved on to describe how their lives had taken a sharp turn for the worse during the bleak years of the Potato Famine. By the second year of the famine, Patrick and Molly had routinely set out at daybreak to search the barren fields, their hands sifting through the dirt in search of something edible. Each night they returned to their sons with barely enough to avoid starvation.

Patrick's voice grew husky as he described watching his children become more and more emaciated. He finally fell silent, reliving a scene that Jack couldn't share.

"You and I aren't so different, lad," he finally said. "I started working my land with great dreams for the future. When lean times came, I met the challenge the only way I knew how, as a gladiator waging my own private battle with fate. Year after year, I kept planting potatoes that came up rotten. In the end, I had to be choosing between certain death or changing my course." He stood silently for several moments before concluding, "History does have a way of repeating itself because you, Jack Green, now find yourself at the same crossroad. You can either hold to the path of a gladiator, or you can open your mind to a better way."

"Is it too late?" Jack asked.

"Well, we'll be hard set to turn things around, make no mistake about that," Patrick warned, "but it can be done."

Jack met Patrick's gaze resolutely. "I want to try. What do I have to do?"

"I'll be needing your signature on this," Patrick said as he rummaged through his golf bag and emerged with a legal document printed in dark green ink and bearing the official seal of the Foundation.

The contract informed Jack that at the striking of each hour, a new trainer would instruct him on one of the nine keys to building a city of influence.

"A city of influence?" Jack asked.

"We'll get to that soon enough. Keep reading," Patrick instructed.

When Jack finished, Patrick pointed to the final line and asked, "Will you read this last bit aloud?"

Jack cleared his throat. "'I hereby agree to suspend judgment and to complete all aspects of the training in full. I understand that failing to do so will result in the death of my business.'"

He looked at Patrick questioningly.

"Your professional life is hanging in the balance," Patrick affirmed. "I'm happy to lend a hand, but I don't waste my time with fence sitters. If you sign this, you will be finishing the training. If you're not ready to pledge yourself to it, 'tis best we say our good-byes now."

Jack put the contract on the table and signed his name. As he laid the pen down, Patrick reached into his pocket and pulled out an ornate key.

Jack came closer. "What is it?" he asked.

"'Tis the first of the nine keys to the city of influence," Patrick said, holding it out to him.

Jack eagerly took the key and examined it. Etched across its surface were the words *Exit the Coliseum*.

"Before you can progress you must break the chains that have kept you a prisoner inside the coliseum," Patrick said. "You must leave the coliseum and never look back."

Patrick took back the key, explaining that Jack would receive his own set at the end of the training. Then, glancing down at his watch, Patrick gave a start.

"Spells and curses, would you look at the time! Are you ready then?"

"For what?" Jack asked, looking around apprehensively.

"To visit an old friend of mine."

5.

The Governor

There is not strength without unity.

—Irish Proverb

A rushing sound filled Jack's ears, and a great wind swept through the room, whipping the edges of his clothing around him and scattering his papers in every direction. Then a second blast hit, but this one was filled with dirt and debris. Choking and coughing, Jack tried to shield his face.

Then, just as quickly as it had begun, the wind stopped and everything was still. When Jack lowered his arms he discovered he was now standing on a dirt path. To his right, the trunks of young trees had been ingeniously threaded together to form a fence that enclosed a small village full of thatched cottages. The pungent scent of burning wood billowed from the chimneys, and Jack noticed that each house had an adjacent garden filled with ripe ears of corn, heads of cabbage, and yellow squash.

The dirt path wound its way beyond the small community, finally disappearing into the distant dunes that bordered a misty blue harbor. Jack could almost taste the salty ocean breeze.

"I welcome you to Plymouth Plantation, Jack Green."

Jack whirled around to see a stocky man wearing a wide-brimmed hat and a dark cloak across his broad shoulders. His simple appearance was a sharp contrast to the deep oranges and reds of the forest behind him.

Jack looked at the man in surprise. "Where am I?" he asked.

"Perhaps a better question is *when* are you. It is the year of our Lord 1621 and this is Plymouth Plantation, later to become part of the Massachusetts Bay Colony. My name is William Bradford."

Jack felt his insides twist in surprise. "Unbelievable," he murmured. "I'm with the pilgrims? You're *Governor* William Bradford?"

"I am indeed. I was chosen to lead our community after our first governor, John Carver, died."

William's strong features radiated such integrity and genuine concern that Jack instantly understood why the Pilgrims had chosen him to be their leader.

"Patrick requested that I be one of your trainers," William said, "to teach you the second key to building a city of influence."

"What's a city of influence?" Jack found himself asking again.

"Come with me," William replied, "and I will show you."

As they passed by one of the cottages, Jack saw a woman roasting a duck over a spit as she kept a watchful eye on her two children. In the fields on the outskirts of the village, they passed several groups of men harvesting crops. Jack and William then climbed up a small rise that overlooked the settlement and sat on two barrels that had been flipped upside down to create makeshift chairs.

"How are you faring after your visit to the coliseum?" William inquired.

"Well, I'll say this much—you guys certainly don't pull any punches when trying to make a point," Jack replied with a shake of his head.

"That may be due to having too many years to improve upon the training," William suggested with a brief smile. "But you must concede that the coliseum plays its part well. I imagine you would be content never to lay eyes on it again?"

"Yes," Jack agreed. "But what's the alternative?"

"Building a city of influence is the only way to escape the coliseum, but to illustrate this, I will need your assistance."

Jack helped William gather piles of stones, twigs and pine needles, and four long branches. William used the branches to outline a large square on top of the dirt. Then using the other materials he began fashioning a miniature city inside the boundaries. Jack watched in fascination as William crafted houses, gardens, roads, fences, and storehouses inside the intricate little city.

Seeing Jack's expression, William shrugged his shoulders and grinned. "I suspect we are defter with our hands than those of your generation."

As he laid the last piece of road, William said, "Every person has a city of influence. Some are small and some are large. Some are beautiful and some . . . shall we say, have fallen into disrepair." Pointing to the city, William continued, "This represents your city of influence, each structure inside of it symbolizing one of your relationships."

William lifted away two of the structures then drew from his pile of rocks to create a new one.

"What happens if two cottages are removed but just one is built?" he asked.

"If it keeps happening, the city will have negative growth," Jack responded.

"And how would that trend affect the value of the town's land and possessions?" William asked.

"They would decrease and eventually become worthless."

William continued to remove cottages as he spoke. "Jack, your city has had negative growth for the past three years. Instead of cultivating new relationships and increasing your population, you have chosen to spend your time battling inside the coliseum. You have left your city unattended, and there are very few residents left to protect your borders." William paused, then looked directly at Jack as he concluded, "To save your business, you must begin investing your time and resources into rebuilding your city. First, you must strengthen your current residents, and then you must work to create an environment to draw in new citizens."

William lifted an ornate key ring from his belt and held out one of the keys. Inscribed on its surface were the words *Decide to Govern*.

Jack was intrigued. "The opposite of a gladiator is a governor?"

"Leaders play two different roles inside their organizations. They are both a mayor and a governor," William said as he threaded the key ring back onto his belt. "All people have a city of influence and act as mayors for their townships. Governors, on the other hand, not only manage their own cities, but have the added responsibility of working to assist those under their leadership to grow and maintain their cities as well. Do you understand?"

"I think so," Jack responded. "You're saying after I learn how to be an effective mayor, I need to teach my staff to do the same?"

William nodded, then asked, "How many merchants would you say survive in your time?"

Jack leaned back against the rough tree trunk, looking up into its gold leaves as he considered the question. "I've seen different numbers. I read one statistic that said over half will go out of business within the first four years."

William nodded. "A large number of the colonies failed to survive in the New World as well. They failed because they arrived on these shores as gladiators instead of governors. By seeing others as opponents to battle and defeat, these individuals either met their end at sword's point or re-treated to their homelands. Our colony survived because it was founded on a different set of principles. As a governor I worked and toiled to *gather* as many new citizens as I could into our cities of influence."

William asked Jack to help him add new structures to the city, and they soon had to expand its borders. When they finally finished, William sat back on his heels, brushed the dirt from his hands and surveyed their work with satisfaction.

"While gladiators fight solely for their own interests," William explained, "governors work to build and cultivate cities that benefit all of the people within them. Governors understand that individual knowledge and resources are never enough to build something great, so they make creating relationships a priority. They always remember that every person inside their organization has a city and that every healthy city significantly increases the company's chances for success. As you work to help all members of your team increase their individual power to influence, Dillon-Parker will begin to grow in ways that will astound you," William concluded.

Jack heard shouts of laughter and looked up to see a group of American Indian braves sitting among several of the Pilgrim children. A little girl was tying a piece of fabric around one of the brave's eyes, and then all of the children jumped to their feet and began shrieking with delight as the young man staggered around trying to catch them.

"There is one of our most important relationships," William said with obvious affection. "One that assisted us far beyond our expectations."

"Who is it?" Jack asked.

"His name is Squanto. He not only taught us how to fertilize the ground so our corn would grow, but he also shared the secrets of trapping and fishing about which we were entirely ignorant. Without him, we wouldn't have survived our second winter."

A Pilgrim man approached Squanto to ask for assistance in communicating with the American Indian brave that stood with him.

"Squanto became our ambassador to the nearby tribes and helped us establish friendly trading relations with them." A cloud seemed to pass over William's expression as he continued. "Many foolishly battled the American Indians instead of seeing them as potential citizens in their cities of influence. Yet what would have become of us if we'd tried, as gladiators, to destroy Squanto instead of expanding our boundaries to include him in our city?"

Jack didn't bother to respond. The answer was obvious.

6.
Self-Made Myths

Pity him who makes his opinions a certainty.

—Irish Proverb

William looked to where the sun had begun to dip below the horizon. "It seems our time together is finished."

As he spoke, the governor's face began to blur. Jack blinked his eyes, trying to clear his vision, but his surroundings eventually faded into blackness.

The first thing he remembered feeling was his body pressing up against something cold and smooth. Opening his eyes, Jack found himself lying on a black-and-white checkered floor that stretched out underneath him like a giant chessboard. Breathing in the musty smell of leather and paper, he stood up and turned full circle. A massive collection of books now surrounded him.

Elaborately carved bookcases stretched upward toward a stained-glass ceiling that depicted the Thanksgiving feast at Plymouth. The bright sunlight refracted through the panes of colored glass and illuminated the entire room. Each bookcase was filled with thousands of leather-bound books sitting in horizontal rows. The volumes seemed identical at first, but when Jack moved closer, he realized that a different person's name was etched into each of the leather bindings.

He walked through an archway into another enormous room and saw a long wooden counter lining its east wall. Behind it sat a woman in a cream business suit sorting several piles of books. Her auburn hair was twisted up off her neck with a pencil.

The woman looked up as he approached. "You must be Jack! Let me be the first to welcome you back to the twenty-first century," she said as she reached over the counter to shake his hand. "I'm Cordelia Ballard and I'll be your next trainer."

"What is this place?" Jack asked.

"It's the National Library of Influence," Cordelia replied. She put down the book in her hand and walked around the counter to join Jack, putting her hand in her pocket and lifting something out. "I have something for you. You will be getting a lot of keys at the end of the training, and I thought you might appreciate a key ring to put them on."

She handed the ring to Jack. On its surface was a circular inscription: *Every Opportunity Has Its Root in a Relationship.*

"Every opportunity?" Jack echoed.

Cordelia looked amused. "That's exactly how I felt the first time I heard it—skeptical. I have a very analytical mind, and that kind of absolute statement didn't sit well with me."

"Yeah, that doesn't sound right to me either," Jack said. "I mean, I understand that the Pilgrims needed relationships to survive, but it doesn't necessarily follow that everyone needs relationships to succeed. Look at self-made people like Walt Disney or Sam Walton."

"Do you really think either of those men succeeded by themselves?" Cordelia asked.

"Well, you don't hear much about anyone else," Jack pointed out.

"You definitely came to the right place," Cordelia replied.

But Jack wasn't ready to leave it at that.

"Okay, relationships probably played a role in their success," he persisted. "Maybe even some of their best opportunities came from other people, but I'm sure there are lots of opportunities that don't have anything to do with relationships. There certainly have been for me."

"Really?" A sparkle came into Cordelia's eyes, and Jack wondered if she were secretly laughing at him. "Like what?"

Jack took a second to think.

"Got one," he announced triumphantly. "My first job out of high school. I answered a want-ad in the paper."

"On the surface I can see how you would think that had nothing to do with relationships," Cordelia replied. She seemed to be choosing her words carefully. "But let me ask you a few questions. How did you find that ad in the paper?"

As Jack thought about it, he realized his father, who devoured the newspaper from cover to cover everyday, had handed him the classified section before he left for work. He had circled several jobs that he thought Jack might qualify for.

"My dad," Jack admitted.

"Tell me about the job," Cordelia said.

"I worked at an auto repair shop," Jack replied.

"And you got that kind of job with no experience?" Cordelia said, her eyebrows lifting in surprise.

"No," Jack admitted reluctantly. "My best friend's dad was an engineer. The three of us used to spend hours in his garage taking apart machinery and putting it back together."

"Did you use your friend's father as a reference?"

Jack said he had.

"We've identified a couple of relationships that played a role in that opportunity, and I guarantee if we kept digging, we could uncover a lot more," Cordelia said. "And just so you know, Sam Walton and Walt Disney are no different. Follow me and I'll show you."

They passed a large number of bookcases as they walked over to the north wing, and Jack observed that each case had a plaque with a different business leader's name engraved on it. He saw book collections for Darwin Smith, Mary Kay Ash, Jack Welch, Ray Kroc, Henry Ford, Mark Cain, Esteé Lauder, Andrea Jung, John Nordstrom, Debbi Fields, Cork Walgreen, Oprah Winfrey, and Jeff Bezos.

When he asked Cordelia about the plaques, she explained that the Foundation had given her a grant to compile the world's largest collection of relationship histories.

"Every volume inside these collections represents a relationship inside that person's city of influence," Cordelia told him. "Having influence is much like having a living library. When governors or mayors have a need, they simply 'check out' the knowledge or resources of the people inside their influence. It naturally follows then that the more books you have in your collection, the better your chances are for success."

Jack tried to wrap his mind around what Cordelia was saying but was still struggling to fully grasp her meaning.

"One way to better understand this principle is to play a game," Cordelia said. "It's a relationship scavenger hunt. Look through the collections and bring me back some books that look interesting."

Jack looked down the long halls in dismay. "Where should I start?"

"You mentioned Walt Disney—his collection is right over there," she said, pointing to a massive collection across the hall.

Jack nodded, and as he walked toward the wooden bookshelves he saw a plaque bearing the words, *Walt Disney Collection*. The collection stretched up several stories, and, curious about what names he'd find at the top, Jack pushed the wooden ladder along its track and climbed up to select a volume.

After exploring several other collections, Jack returned with a stack of books. Sitting in the armchair across from Cordelia, he pushed them across the low wooden table between them.

"What do we have here?" Cordelia asked, leaning forward to examine the spines of Jack's selections. She then picked up the book on the top and said, "Let's start with *Ub Iwerks* from the *Walt Disney Collection*."

"That's one unusual name," Jack commented.

Cordelia agreed and opened the book. She showed Jack the sketches of different cartoon characters that filled the inside cover.

"Walt Disney wasn't a top-notch animator, and he knew it," Cordelia explained. "So, using all his powers of persuasion, Walt set out to convince his friend and former partner, Ub Iwerks, to leave a high-paying job and relocate halfway across the country. He was successful, and Ub became the studio's first chief animator."

Cordelia explained that the studio experienced some early success with a cartoon character named Oswald the Rabbit, but then disaster struck. While Walt was in New York renegotiating their contract, his distributor informed Walt that not only was he taking Oswald away from him, but he had also secretly recruited all Walt's animators to come work for him.

"All the animators except for one, that is. Even though Ub knew that staying with Walt meant that he was now a staff of one, he refused to desert his friend. On the train ride back to California, Walt had an idea for a new character, but it was Ub who brought him to life."

Cordelia looked up at Jack mischievously. "Any guesses who that turned out to be?"

"No way! Mickey Mouse?" Jack asked.

Cordelia nodded. "Do you see where the principle 'Every opportunity has its root in a relationship' starts getting its teeth? Without Ub, there might have never been a Mickey Mouse."

Closing the book and placing it back on the table, Cordelia observed, "Ub Iwerks is a pretty important volume inside Walt's collection, wouldn't you say? And he's only one of thousands of key relationships inside Walt's city of influence."

Cordelia picked up the second book entitled *George Billingsly* that Jack had found inside the *Sam Walton Collection*. As she flipped through the pages she explained that Wal-Mart and Proctor and Gamble had always had a typical vendor/retailer relationship, with the buyers and salesmen constantly haggling without any communication between corporate officers.

Lou Pritchett, a vice-president of Proctor and Gamble, wanted to change all that. He phoned a lifelong friend, George Billingsly (who was also a close friend of Sam's), for help, and George arranged for the three of them to take a two-day canoe trip. As they floated down the river, Sam and Lou got the chance to talk about their businesses and soon realized that working independently of each other was costing them both a lot of money. After they got back, the two men assembled the top officers of both companies for a two-day retreat. Three months later they forged the P&G/Wal-Mart team. The systems they developed for sharing information ended up transforming the way they did business.

"This is amazing," Jack said. "I can't believe I've never heard of any of these people."

"Just wait until you hear this next one," Cordelia said, picking up the volume entitled *Tim Patterson*.

While browsing through the Bill Gate's section, Jack had stumbled on the collection of Paul Allen, Microsoft's co-founder, and had selected this book.

"When IBM came to Microsoft and offered Microsoft the opportunity to provide the computer language for IBM's new personal computer, Paul Allen and Bill Gates were ecstatic," Cordelia told him. "This was the chance of a lifetime for their young company—one they couldn't afford to lose. But when IBM's negotiations with the leading operating-system provider fell through, IBM came to Microsoft and insisted they also find them an operating system or the deal was off."

Cordelia explained that Microsoft specialized in computer languages, not operating systems, and that the partnership was in real jeopardy. Luckily for Microsoft, Paul Allen had a friend named Tim Patterson who had created his own operating system while working at Seattle Computers. Seattle Computers agreed to sell the operating system to Microsoft for less than $100,000 and Microsoft presented it to IBM to seal their partnership. Tim's name for his system was originally the "Quick and Dirty Operating System," or QDOS, for short. Microsoft later changed it to MSDOS.

"Are you serious?" Jack asked, his jaw dropping. "Paul Allen just said, 'Don't worry about it. I know a guy with a spare operating system'?"

Cordelia nodded, "Crazy, huh? Think about it, Jack. If Tim Patterson's volume hadn't been inside Paul Allen's city of influence, there may have been no Microsoft/IBM partnership. That opportunity helped put Microsoft on the map."

"Wow!" Jack said under his breath, slowly shaking his head. He'd always viewed founders and CEOs of major corporations as coming from a different breed, assuming their success was exclusively the result of their own relentless effort and a far-reaching vision. Now, realizing they'd built their empires through hundreds of key relationships, they seemed a little more human.

Cordelia began to run through the rest of the titles.

"When Phil Knight needed a logo for his new running shoes, he asked an art student he knew named Carolyn Davidson if she would design something. They later affectionately dubbed her logo 'the swoosh.'"

Cordelia then explained how Esteé Lauder's uncle, John Schotz, had taught his niece the secrets of skin care at a very young age, and how, together, they'd concocted a snowy cream that made skin feel like silk. That cream became the foundation of the billion-dollar Esteé Lauder empire.

Picking up the volume from the Google section entitled *David Cheriton*, Cordelia explained, "When Larry Page and Sergey Brin needed funding to turn their doctoral project into an actual company, they turned to their Stanford faculty advisor, David Cheriton. He connected them with a friend who also happened to be a legendary Silicon Valley investor. They arranged an early-morning meeting on David's front porch, and by the end of their conversation, David's friend wrote Larry and Sergey a check for $100,000 and Google was born."

"*Tommie Wilck*," Cordelia said, picking up the last volume. "Oh, I like this one."

She explained how, after years of effort, Walt Disney had finally acquired the screen rights for the book *Mary Poppins* and needed to find an actress to play the lead role. They brainstormed and discarded different ideas until Walt's secretary, Tommie Wilck, suggested a young actress she'd recently seen on Broadway named Julie Andrews.

"And the rest is history. *Mary Poppins* made $44 million in its first release. It also garnered 13 Academy Award nominations, one of which went to Hollywood newcomer Julie Andrews for best actress."

Cordelia placed the book on top of the stack and said, "Jack, our culture constantly celebrates the achievements of individuals, but no one has ever built something meaningful without the help of others. Wal-Mart wasn't built by Sam Walton alone. Without hundreds of key relationships, Bill Gates would probably be teaching math classes. The truth is that we all need other people to play a role in our story."

"Okay, okay, I give up," Jack said, raising his hands in defeat. "Self-made success is a myth, just like Santa Claus."

"Maybe it's better if we save that discussion for a later time," Cordelia replied, flashing him a bright smile.

As he helped Cordelia carry the books back to the sorting counter, Jack realized how seldom he'd considered the contributions of other people to his life.

As if reading his thoughts, Cordelia asked, "Would you like to see your collection?"

Jack looked around eagerly. "Mine? You have a section for me?"

"My newest one," Cordelia said over her shoulder. She motioned for Jack to follow her down the corridor. They trekked to the other side of the sprawling north wing and finally stopped before a wall modestly stocked with several hundred books.

"Not exactly Walt Disney, but here it is. The *Jack Green Collection*," Cordelia announced with a flourish. "You will find individual volumes for each of your friends, family, coworkers, clients, vendors and any other category you can think of. Each significant relationship is represented in there somewhere."

As Jack scanned through the names, Cordelia handed him a clipboard and a pen.

"Do you remember William explaining how governors seek to actively increase the population of their cities of influence?"

"Yes," Jack said.

"Well, every year I make a wish list for the books I'd like to add to the library, and I want you to do something similar. Think of ten people you don't currently know but would like to add to your city of influence this year."

Jack took the clipboard and sat down at a nearby table, carefully thinking through who he would include if he could have them for the asking. He began writing, until finally he handed the clipboard back to Cordelia.

She read through the list and inquired about several of the names.

"You listed Will Clay first. Tell me about him."

"Will Clay is a partner at a national law firm called Clay and Chagall," Jack explained. "Their firm needs a new look and they know it. We've been trying to convince them to let us create their new brand for almost two years now, and I heard our top sales person finally got through to him the other day, so it looks promising."

"He'll do nicely as a practice case," Cordelia murmured thoughtfully, circling his name.

"What?" Jack asked curiously, wondering if he'd heard correctly.

"Never mind," Cordelia said, shaking her head. Then, nudging his arm, she said, "Jack, let's play the game one more time. Find a name you don't know."

Jack looked confused. "But this is my collection. Shouldn't I know all of the names?"

"Just try it," she insisted.

Jack got up and slowly skimmed through the book titles, then he reached down and pulled a book out from the bottom shelf.

"*Ted Jacobson?* Who's he?" Jack asked, looking down at the book in confusion.

"Ted Jacobson," Cordelia said, wrinkling her forehead reflectively. She took the book from Jack and started flipping through the pages. "Oh, right. He's the manager of the Kingpin Bowling Alley."

"Oh, that Ted." Jack stopped to think. "I don't think I ever knew his last name."

"Some people think he's a little unusual, don't they?" Cordelia asked, holding open a page that had a full-length photo of Ted. He was tall and lanky and his sandy blond hair fell into his eyes.

"Yeah, I guess," Jack replied. "A lot of people don't give him the time of day, but he's actually a really great guy."

He searched his memory for opportunities that came from Ted, but drew a blank.

Cordelia finally asked him if he remembered playing on a winter bowling league. Jack nodded; he'd had the top score at one of the tournament games. Suddenly, it clicked.

"The Oak Grove Community Bank team!" Jack exclaimed, throwing up his hands in triumph. "Ted asked me if I would fill an empty spot on their team and that's where I met Murray."

Cordelia pointed out that Murray was not only one of Jack's best friends, but also one of his most important business associates.

She pulled Murray's book off the shelf and added, "He was instrumental in getting the loans you needed to finance Dillon-Parker, and he also introduced you to another key business relationship."

Jack instantly realized who Cordelia was referring to.

"Monty. I met Monty at one of Murray's new-client lunches." Jack was shocked he'd never made the connection before.

"You have Monty, partner and half-owner of your business, because of Murray. And you know Murray because of Ted Jacobson," Cordelia pointed out.

"I should probably send him a thank-you note or something," Jack said, trying to remember the last time he'd talked to Ted.

Cordelia retrieved three more volumes from a nearby table, and presented them to Jack. Etched onto their leather spines were the names of *Patrick O'Flannery*, *William Bradford*, and *Cordelia Ballard*.

"Go ahead and put them on the shelf, Jack. You'd better get used to adding new residents to your city of influence."

After Jack shelved the books, Cordelia led him up a nearby flight of stairs to a small alcove. From it, Jack could see shelves of books sprawling out in every direction.

As they stood side by side, looking out over the collections, Cordelia said, "Jack, the purpose of this library is to help you understand a principle that isn't taught in school. The principle is this: individual resources will never be enough. Success in business swings on the hinge of a thousand key relationships, and if you want your business to be listed among the giants, you must add volumes to your collection every single day."

A bell signaled the passing of the hour, and Cordelia smiled up at Jack. "Well now, George Bailey, it looks like you've realized what a wealthy man you are."

"Yeah, it's a wonderful life, Clarence," Jack replied with a wry grin.

7.

Bricks

There's no need to fear the wind if your haystacks are tied down.

—Irish Proverb

Jack's body suddenly went numb, and he looked down to discover it was slowly fading away. He reappeared in a new location, directly in the path of two men carrying small trees in burlap sacks. But like a river moving past a boulder in its way, the workers simply sidestepped him and joined the large landscaping crew busily working on the finishing touches of a beautiful new home.

Jack spotted Patrick and went over to join him.

"You might want to consider creating a warning system that lets your students know when they're about to travel through time and space," Jack complained as he got closer. "Every time it happens I think I've died."

"Just remember not to go toward the light, lad," Patrick responded with a grin. "Well then, tell me about your trip to the library."

"It was amazing," Jack responded, instantly enthusiastic. "I could've spent an entire day there."

"Cordelia does have a lovely way of telling a story," Patrick agreed.

Looking at the house, Jack told Patrick, "Construction sites are a kind of hobby for me. Can we have a look around?"

Patrick agreed and they made their way to the backyard where another crew was installing a large wooden deck.

"This contractor is really good," Jack commented as he admired the dark brick and stucco exterior. "After they foreclose on my house, I'll have to hire him to build my new five-hundred square foot apartment," Jack told Patrick, only half kidding.

"Then you two best be meeting," Patrick replied.

Entering the kitchen through the back door, Jack saw two men standing there. One of the men let out an infectious laugh, and Jack found himself wishing he could share the joke. Patrick closed the door behind them, and when the man saw them he immediately excused himself.

"Jack, I'd like you to be meeting Ron Baker," Patrick said as the man joined them. "He builds more custom homes than any other contractor in the valley."

"Well, if I do, it's all because of this little redheaded monster," Ron said, playfully jabbing Patrick. "It's nice to meet you, Jack, although I can't say much for your choice of company. This guy is likely to drive you up the wall with all of his popping in and popping out." Ron said, making little popping noises with his mouth.

Jack laughed and said, "I think I'm going to like you, Ron."

Patrick looked back and forth between Ron and Jack, clearly worried. "I may have been a wee bit daft agreeing to let you do this part of the training, Ron."

"I'll be good," Ron said, raising his arm in the Scout's honor sign. "I promise not to break any of your precious relationship rules."

Ron then pushed himself up on the counter and began asking Jack questions about his training so far. He was so genuinely interested that Jack found himself telling him about his family and business as well.

Patrick interrupted them, "Not to throw a spanner into the works, lads, but we've some business to attend to."

"Oh, all right, then," Ron said with a sigh. "Work, work, work. That's all you ever think about."

Ron picked up a book from the counter and handed it to Jack.

"Does this look familiar?" Ron asked.

Three fat pigs stared up at Jack from the cover.

"Yeah it does," he said in surprise. "This is my daughter's favorite book."

"It's mine, too," Ron said. "But today we're going to be putting a little different spin on it. Are you ready?"

"Ready for what?" Jack asked suspiciously. He had recently acquired a healthy distrust of that question.

"I'm going to tell you the story of the three little pigs," Ron explained. "Or to be more accurate, I am going to make you the story."

Jack's body suddenly pulled and contracted then began spinning violently. The next thing he knew, he was staring straight into the snout of a pig.

The pig pulled itself up onto its hind legs and spoke. "Welcome to your worst nightmare," it growled.

"Ron? You're a pig!" Jack squealed.

"Look who's talking," Ron replied.

Jack looked down to see soft pink skin and cloven hooves, and let out a loud snort. "You have got to be kidding! This training program is way over the top."

"If I were you, I would straighten up and do the two-legged thing," Ron suggested. "It kind of creeps me out if you *act* like a pig, too."

"Sorry, I guess I left my *Pig Etiquette for Dummies* book at home," Jack shot back as he worked himself up onto two legs.

"Give it a chance. This actually ended up being one of my favorite parts of the training," Ron said with a happy sigh. Then his forehead wrinkled slightly. "Of course, that was after I got used to the wolf trying to kill me."

At the mention of a wolf, Jack looked around nervously as Ron continued to speak.

"Welcome to straw. If you haven't figured it out, you're one of the three little pigs, and this is the famous house of straw," Ron announced with a flourish. "In this version of the story, straw represents price."

Ron leaned up against the wall, and one of his hoofs slipped through. After extricating himself, he observed, "This pig didn't choose a very stable building material, did he? Why do you think he decided to use straw?"

"What?" Jack asked, pulling his eyes away from the walls of the hut. "Um, well probably because it was cheap and fast, and he wanted to get a roof over his head as fast as possible."

"Exactly! People usually build their businesses on price for the same reasons. They're looking for quick and easy results," Ron explained. "Can you think of a time when your company chose to compete solely on price?"

Jack remembered that just last week the studio had picked up a national account by cutting their normal rate by thirty percent.

"To be honest, we won't make a dime," Jack admitted with a grimace. "We're hoping they'll like our work enough that we'll gradually be able to increase the price."

"That's a risky way to build a business," Ron observed.

Jack started to justify himself, but Ron put up a hand. "Don't misunderstand. I know fair pricing is important, but you'll never be able to build a stable business around it." Ron then leaned back against the wall and continued. "We live in a world where customer options are endless. With the click of a mouse your clients can find your competitors in 50 states and 100 countries. It might be different if you were selling soup or gasoline, but in a service business like yours, competing solely on price is usually a death sentence."

Jack knew Ron was right. Dillon-Parker wasn't going to survive much longer if they continued competing on price alone.

Outside the walls, Jack heard a scratching sound and heavy panting. Suddenly, a huge gust of wind blew the door, roof, and walls into heaps of rubble. From his huddled position Jack looked up to see an enormous wolf bearing down on him, its sharp fangs exposed.

"Run, Jack, run!" Ron shouted.

Jack's short legs scrambled forward and he bolted after Ron. The wolf was so close that he could feel its warm breath against his backside. Jack was almost certain Patrick wouldn't allow him to be eaten during his training sessions, but he wasn't going to risk being wrong. Jack leapt into a nearby stick shelter and slammed the door shut. The wolf let out a piercing howl, and Jack could see flashes of its black fur through the cracks in the wood as it paced back and forth in front of the hut.

"What happened to 'my chinny chin chin' and all of that?" Jack managed to ask between gasps of air.

"I warned you this version would be a little bit different. In business, you don't always receive notice before the roof caves in," Ron replied.

Ron trotted over to the wall and pulled out one of the sticks with his mouth. He brought it over to Jack, dropping it on the dirt floor in front of him.

"Jack, why do you think the second pig decided to build his house out of sticks instead of straw?"

Jack was still nervously eyeing the doorway, but finally replied, "He was probably thinking more long term. Straw would be easier, but sticks would last longer and be more stable."

Jack couldn't help but feel a faint glow of pride. He'd come up with a relatively intelligent answer even when his bloody death waited just outside the door. Then the wolf let out another shrill howl and Jack shivered.

"Sticks represent performance," Ron said, who didn't seem the least bit ruffled. "When people realize that their business isn't going to survive competing solely on price, they usually start looking for ways to separate themselves from their competition. Those that choose to build with sticks understand that a loyal customer will pay more for an experience they can trust. For example, where did you go on your last vacation?"

"Disneyland."

When Ron asked him why they'd chosen to go there, Jack shrugged like the answer should be obvious. "Because I knew my family was guaranteed to have a great time. It's the Magic Kingdom, after all."

"Exactly! You knew without question that Disneyland would perform at the level you expected and were willing to pay for that luxury. They have phenomenal stick systems," Ron explained. "Can you think of a client who is loyal to Dillon-Parker because of your performance?"

Jack thought this over, then told Ron about Rebar Medical. Their previous agency had missed several deadlines, and during their search for a more reliable firm they'd discovered Dillon-Parker.

"I don't think we've missed a single deadline," Jack finished, but he still felt a gnawing worry inside his stomach. "Why do I get the feeling we're still not safe in sticks?"

As he spoke, a gust of wind sent sticks flying everywhere and the chase was on again. Every few steps, Jack was certain that the wolf's jaws were going to wrap around his hind legs, but somehow he managed to stay just out of reach. He lost sight of Ron as he zigzagged through hollow logs and leapt over small hedges, but his survival instinct kept him moving. Finally, he spotted a brick house and, with another burst of speed, sprinted toward it. He slid through the entrance on his haunches and then turned to slam the door shut.

"Welcome back, lad."

His chest still heaving, Jack turned to face Patrick. They were standing in the entryway of the house they'd started in. Suddenly, there was a knock on the door behind him.

"Hello, little pigs. Can I come in?" a deep voice growled.

"Only if you want me to punch your chinny chin chin!" Jack yelled through the door. Furious, he whirled on Patrick. "You guys are completely nuts! I never should have signed that stupid contract."

"Calm down, now, lad," Patrick said soothingly, as he opened the door and let Ron in.

The contractor had changed back into his human form and his face was red with suppressed laughter.

By this point, Jack realized that he, too, was human again, and muttered, "Fine, but no more funny stuff."

"I'm sorry to put you through that," Patrick said, "but this teaching method tends to weave the threads of the principle into your mind so they hold fast. You'll be thanking me for it later."

"Yeah, much later," Ron hooted.

A few rolls of carpet had been left in the living room and the three men settled themselves on them.

Ron continued where he'd left off. "The third building material, as you've probably guessed, is bricks. Bricks represent the relationships inside of your city of influence, and they are the only building material guaranteed to keep your business safe from the attacks of the wolf. As you experienced, performance has the same weakness as price. What happens when your competition has comparable performance?"

"People usually go with who they know," Jack responded, thinking back to several recent accounts where that very thing had happened. He couldn't blame them, though; Jack knew if he could get comparable price and performance, he always preferred working with people he liked and trusted.

"You're right, Jack. When two competitors both have fair prices and excellent performance then the relationship becomes the deciding factor. And the more expensive the service, the more relevant the relationship becomes," Ron explained.

"Where do you do your banking, lad?" Patrick asked.

"Oak Grove Community," Jack said, startled at the abrupt change of subject.

Patrick asked him if he would ever do his banking anywhere else.

"Not as long as Murray is with them," Jack replied.

"Exactly!" Patrick declared. "That relationship is equivalent to a brick."

Ron picked up the picture book and began leafing through its pages. "Jack, why do you think this story has been told for so many centuries?"

Jack spoke slowly, working out his thoughts as he talked. "Because it teaches us that building something strong is worth the investment, even if others are building things that take much less time and effort."

"Increasing the population of your city and elevating your level of relationships won't happen overnight," Ron said, "but like the third little pig, you'll discover that the rewards of building with bricks far outweigh the costs."

Drawing out his key ring, Ron showed one of the keys to Jack. "And so we come to the third key to building a city of influence."

Engraved on the key's surface was *Recognize Bricks Trump.*

"Remember, if price and performance are equal, then the level of relationship will trump. The reason you are consistently losing opportunities and accounts is because your competition is predictably trumping each of your hands with a higher relationship card. In other words, they have more bricks than you."

Relationship Arrogance

The raggy colt often makes a handsome horse.

—Irish Proverb

"Oh, I *am* good," Ron announced as the alarm on his wristwatch began to beep "I've got this thing down to the second."

As he spoke, the brick house evaporated around them, and Jack found himself back in his den. Glad to be home even for a few minutes, he sank back into the soft leather of his chair, feeling inspired, confused, and frustrated all at the same time.

Reviewing his business career, Jack recalled the many times he'd acted like a gladiator and the occasional times where he'd been more like a governor. As he began dissecting his business strategies—placing them into the straw, stick, and brick categories—he was disappointed to find he had no effective systems for building bricks.

What if this really is the answer? Jack asked himself, feeling one of his pounding headaches coming on.

Part of him didn't want it to be. Relationships took time, and time was the one thing he didn't have. Jack had always prided himself on being a business pragmatist, patterning his life after his favorite quote in *The Godfather*, "It's not personal, it's just business." Trading in all his hard-nosed business practices for a bunch of touchy feely relationship principles seemed to fly in the face of everything he'd always believed in.

As he thought this, he felt a sharp spasm of pain shoot through his heart.

"Ow!" Jack cried, pressing down on his chest to ease the throbbing. His vision began to blur. Then everything went dark.

The next thing he was aware of was a heavy pressure on his tongue and a sudden burst of light in his eyes.

"Say ahhh," a voice directed.

"Whaaaaa," Jack replied, gagging on the tongue depressor.

The light blinding his eyes switched off, and when the purple spots cleared, Jack discovered he was now sitting on the white paper of an examination table. The operator of the tongue depressor stood before him, dressed in green scrubs, her wiry black hair tied back from her brown skin.

She scrawled a few notations on a clipboard and said, "Now then, Mr. Green—may I call you Jack?"

"Sure," Jack said, pulling his eyes away from a nearby canister of hypodermic syringes.

"My name is Dr. Angela Peterman and I'm your next trainer," she said, shaking his hand. "It's a pleasure to meet you, though I do wish it was under more favorable circumstances."

This sounded ominous, and the thin paper crackled beneath Jack as he shifted nervously.

"I'm afraid I have some bad news for you," the doctor continued. "You're suffering from a severe case of RA."

Jack felt the blood drain out of his face, and he braced himself for the worst. "I knew something was wrong. Is it serious?"

"For your business, it definitely can be," the doctor affirmed.

"What is it?" Jack asked, struggling to keep his voice steady.

The doctor suggested that he take a seat on one of the more comfortable chairs that lined the perimeter of the examination room. She waited until he was settled before continuing.

"RA stands for Relationship Arrogance, and although common, it can be deadly," Angela said. "I could give you a highly-technical explanation, but I think it'll make more sense if I use an example."

Angela directed Jack's attention to a dark-paneled x-ray box on the wall that had a large negative clipped to it. When Angela turned on the backlight it revealed a photograph of a group of people sitting around a table eating lunch. Recognizing himself in the picture, Jack realized that it had been taken at the Oak Grove Entrepreneur's Group. He had attended one of their events earlier that week hoping to make some new high level contacts for the studio.

Popping the top off a black marker, Angela handed it to Jack. "I want you to circle the three people you were focusing on at this lunch."

Jack circled three people in the photograph. Two were potential clients and the third was a possible supplier.

"Why did you choose them?" Angela asked.

"I thought they would be valuable business contacts," Jack responded, making a mental note to dig out their business cards and follow up with them when he got back.

Angela uncapped another marker—this one red—and crossed out the other five individuals. She pointed to one, a balding, middle-aged man with round-rimmed glasses who sat next to Jack at the table.

"What about him?" she asked. "Why didn't you take the time to get to know him?"

Jack looked at the man's face, trying to remember who he was. "He's with a small dot-com," Jack finally said, shrugging his shoulders dismissively. "They can't afford us yet."

"Did you not like him?" Angela persisted. "His name is David Edwards, by the way."

"He seemed nice enough," Jack said, a note of defensiveness creeping into his voice. "He reminded me a little of my Uncle Mac."

Angela made no comment, but continued to gaze at Jack steadily.

When the silence became uncomfortable, Jack said, "I was there to network and get new clients. I didn't want to waste all my time talking to someone who couldn't help me grow my business."

Tapping Jack's chest with the marker in her hand, Angela said, "So you're basically saying that he didn't have what you wanted. But are you aware of anything that *he* needed?"

Jack looked back at the picture of David Edwards, trying to remember their short conversation.

"Yeah, I guess it crossed my mind to introduce him to my neighbor Jerry," Jack said. "He owns a company that invests in small technology start-ups, and I overheard David say he was looking for a round of funding."

Nodding, Angela asked, "So why didn't you help him by offering to make the introduction?"

"I was trying to set appointments with the others," Jack said.

Angela apparently didn't realize how close to bankruptcy his business was.

"The definition of Relationship Arrogance is prioritizing relationships based on a forecasted return on investment," Angela said. She turned off the backlight and the picture faded into the dark panel. "You prioritized people based on your maximum return that day, didn't you?"

Without waiting for an answer, Angela pulled out a CAT scan of Jack's upper body and pointed to his chest area. "The infection started in your heart and has corrupted your vision. When you meet people, you prioritize their worth based on whether you think they can help you achieve your immediate objectives."

Jack opened his mouth to protest that this wasn't true, but as he tried to cite examples to argue his case, he found himself at a loss.

"But I can't build relationships with everyone," he finally responded. "That's just not possible."

"I'm not saying that you should build a relationship with every person you meet," Angela said. "I'm saying that the way you judge people affects your ability to build a relationship with them, and that it's arrogant to make assumptions before having any meaningful interaction."

Angela stood up and walked over to the opposite end of the examination room, standing next to a metal vault that Jack could've sworn hadn't been there a moment before.

"On the other side of this door are the results of David Edward's influence-scan," she said, pulling out a small card with a magnetic strip. "I've gotten clearance for us to go inside."

Angela slid the card through a small electronic scanner, and the light on the handle flashed green as the thick door swung open on its huge hinges. As they entered the cavernous room, Jack saw hundreds of three-dimensional holographic images, each one actively engaged in some kind of activity: the images were talking on their cell phones, driving their cars, sitting in business meetings, working at their desks.

"What is this place?" Jack asked.

"It's a visual representation of David Edward's city of influence. Every person he has a relationship with is in here somewhere."

Wandering through the room, Jack stopped in front of a woman who was waterskiing and called out, "He knows Jane Baird! She used to be my real estate agent. Wow, this place is like a funhouse on steroids."

"Jack," Angela called out from the other side of the room. "Come over here and see this."

Jack made his way through the maze of holograms, walking past a couple sitting hunched down in their seats in a movie theater, their terrified eyes glued to the screen and past a woman interviewing a nervous-looking young man for a job. He found Angela standing next to the image of a man talking to a bank teller.

"Jack, allow me to introduce you to someone," Angela said with a flourish. "I don't think you've met Will Clay."

"Will Clay?" Jack repeated, shocked.

Angela permitted herself a small smile. "I spoke with Cordelia about your relationship wish list before you arrived. Will Clay is David Edward's neighbor and has been one of his best friends for years. In fact, they play golf every week."

Jack closed his eyes and groaned softly.

"Relationship Arrogance tends to be the principle that cuts straight to the heart," Angela said, patting Jack's shoulder sympathetically.

She steered Jack out of the influence-scan and back into the stark examination room. "I think you'd better sit down," she suggested, a worried look on her face.

"I'm an idiot," Jack said, burying his face in his hands.

"Yes, you are. But I wouldn't feel too bad about it because so is almost everyone else."

Angela opened the drawer underneath the hypodermic needles, and drew out a set of keys. She showed one to Jack who read the inscription: *Avoid Relationship Arrogance.*

"Self-interest is the sole motivation of gladiators, and if they can't forecast a quick return on a relationship, they discard the relationship and move on. But what they don't understand is that every person has hidden influence they can't see."

Jack replayed the lunch in his mind, wondering how he would've done things differently if only he could've seen David Edward's connection with Will Clay.

Angela seemed to guess what he was thinking. "At this point, I should warn you of another pitfall. When you begin to understand that everyone has hidden influence, there's a temptation to build a relationship simply to access it. Building relationships with this motivation is not a good idea, either, because you're still forecasting a return on your investment. People can sense that kind of thing and will instinctively distrust you."

Angela picked up a pad of paper and scribbled on it. "I'm going to refer you to one of our specialists—our very best in fact. He can usually treat even the most serious cases of Relationship Arrogance."

She ripped off the slip of paper with practiced efficiency and handed the prescription to Jack. As she did this, Jack heard the printer in the corner come on and spit out a piece of paper.

"Oh, I almost forgot. You also need your receipt," she said, picking up the paper and handing it to him.

Looking at the total, Jack started to panic. "This is over eight hundred thousand dollars! I can't pay this!"

"Don't worry. It's a receipt, not a bill. And you've already paid it in full," Angela reassured him. "That's the amount Relationship Arrogance has already cost your company in lost revenue. Unfortunately, we have no way of calculating the personal costs, but I can assure you those are usually even more severe."

9

Just Because

What is in the marrow is hard to take out of the bone.

—Irish Proverb

Double-checking the total on the receipt, Jack sensed he'd changed locations once again. Looking up, he found himself standing beside Patrick in the center of a shopping mall. They were waiting near the front of a long line of eager children and their parents. The line wound through a white picket fence enclosing nine mechanical reindeer and two giant candy canes.

Jack looked around incredulously. "What happened to October and November? I swear it was September this morning."

Patrick shook his head. "You've already traveled back hundreds of years tonight. Don't tell me a few months is going to put you in a state."

As he said this, the line moved, and Patrick nudged Jack forward.

"Wait a second. What are we doing?" Jack asked, stepping back and looking at Patrick suspiciously.

"We're going to your appointment with the specialist," Patrick said, pointing to the raised platform where Santa Claus sat inside his sleigh, his snowy beard spilling out over his red velvet suit. "You're sure to like him. The man's a saint."

Jack felt like he'd jumped into a Christmas TV special, complete with all the clichéd trimmings. He slapped a hand against his forehead and started to laugh.

"You're putting me on, right? As if turning me into a pig wasn't enough, now Santa's going to help me save my business? And look, Rudolph and Frosty are here, too!" Jack said in mock celebration, pointing to the fiberglass figurines in the Christmas display.

A passing marching band suddenly struck up "Deck the Halls," and people dressed up as gingerbread cookies began handing out gifts to the crowd. The line instantly dissolved as everyone left to follow the parade, leaving Jack standing alone in front.

"Santa," Patrick said, pushing Jack forward a little, "I'm not sure this young lad remembers knowing you, so it'll be my pleasure to reintroduce you. Jack, I'd like you to meet Kris Kringle."

Still shaking his head in disbelief, Jack looked up into Kris's brilliant blue eyes. Their gaze locked and Jack felt a flood of childlike happiness sweep through him.

"Well, well if it isn't Jack Green! It's a pleasure to see you again," said Kris, his deep voice ringing out as he spoke.

A memory flitted at the edges of Jack's consciousness, but when he tried to pin it down, it slipped away.

Kris stroked his beard and began to chuckle. "I'm afraid you're going to have to climb up here to talk with me. Don't worry, you can sit there," he said pointing to the vacant space across from him on the sleigh. "You're getting a little big for my knee."

Jack felt embarrassment surge through his rapidly reddening cheeks, but in his mind's eye he saw his signature at the bottom of the training contract and he pulled himself up into the sleigh.

Kris's voice softened with sympathy. "This has been an especially rough year for you, hasn't it?"

Jack nodded, his eyes downcast.

"So, what can I do for you? I'm at your service," Kris said, holding out his hands, indicating his readiness.

"Anything?" Jack said, looking up at Kris in surprise.

"I'll do my best," Kris promised.

Jack looked over at Patrick doubtfully, and Patrick nodded encouragingly. "Go ahead, lad. You know what you've been wanting."

Suddenly, what Cordelia had said about Will Clay popped into Jack's mind. *He'll do as a practice case.* Wasn't that what she'd muttered under her breath?

"I've wanted to get the Clay & Chagall account. I think it might help save my business," Jack told him.

Kris let out a low whistle and leaned back against the shellacked backboard of the sleigh. "That's a pretty tall order. Tell me more about it."

As Jack described Dillon-Parker's struggles, he had the distinct impression Kris cleared every other thought out of his head to devote his full attention to what Jack was telling him. When he'd finished, Kris asked Jack for the prescription Dr. Angela had given him.

Kris skimmed through it, then turned to Patrick. "My friend, it's time for my supper, and I'm very tired of the Corn Dog Palace. I've actually been craving some of your wife's Irish stew."

"Molly'll be delighted to have you both!" Patrick exclaimed. "And she'll feed you a feast that'll hold you through the longest day."

The next thing Jack knew, he was looking up at a cluster of copper kettles hanging from the iron ceiling rods of an elaborate kitchen. On the counter in front of him sat large piles of round potatoes, leafy lettuce, and fat orange carrots.

Kris cleared his throat and Jack followed his gaze to where a petite woman was standing on a squat, three-legged stool, reaching for something on the top shelf of a cupboard. Alerted to their arrival, Molly turned and stared at the three of them, dumbfounded. Then, letting out a wail, she lit into her husband.

"Glory be, Patrick! You need to be warning me when you're bringing home guests. I'm a sight to be seen!"

Brushing back an auburn curl from her glistening forehead, Molly tried, unsuccessfully, to smooth it back into her bun.

"It's my fault," Kris broke in, stepping forward to take the blame. "I was craving some of your divine stew. I hope I'm not putting you out."

Molly instantly softened. She gave the old man a hug, then stood back and looked him over. "Sure, and your looking like you haven't eaten in ages. I'll be warming up some supper directly."

Turning to Jack, she took both of his hands in her tiny ones, her eyes bright with tears. "And Jack! My, but you do have the look of your great-grandfather to you," she commented, her eyes never leaving Jack's face. "It's glad I am to finally meet you. Patrick's been telling me what a quick learner you're turning out to be now that the famous Green stubbornness is wearing off."

Jack laughed. "Thank you . . . I think."

Patrick took charge of setting the table, and as Jack helped him put out the knives and forks, Jack stole a quick peek out the kitchen window. He saw a shady lane filled with beautiful brick homes, but before he could inquire about their exact location, he was distracted by a mouthwatering smell. Molly had lifted the lid off the large pot sitting on the stove, and as its succulent blend of bacon, garlic, and spices wafted through the kitchen, Jack's stomach let out a growl.

"I see you've inherited the Green appetite as well," Molly observed with a laugh. She dipped her wooden spoon into the stew and tasted it critically. "Not my finest, but it'll have to do. Let's get some nourishment into you."

Kris insisted he didn't want Molly to open the formal dining room, so the group gathered around the cozy kitchen table to eat. The dinner conversation centered on Jack's training thus far, and as Molly passed out generous helpings of stew and thick slices of brown soda bread, Jack acted out his first meeting with Patrick. He mimicked his trainer so perfectly that tears of laughter were soon running down everyone's cheeks, including Patrick's.

When they finished, Patrick and Molly began to clear the table, insisting that they would clean up, and that Jack and Kris should use the time to talk.

"Courtesy is no more important than wisdom," Patrick said firmly, pushing Jack back in his seat as he attempted to clear his plate. "Kris has things to tell you, things to say."

As the two men sat among the remains of the feast, Kris sighed contentedly and let out his belt a couple of notches. He then drew out Angela's prescription and read over it again.

"Did Angela explain that the occurrence of Relationship Arrogance is especially high among gladiators?" he asked.

"No, but that would make sense," Jack replied, remembering how every thought in his head had been riveted on his own survival when he'd been battling in the coliseum.

"People can usually spot a gladiator a mile away because they view others as human bank machines whose sole purpose is dispensing money and opportunities to them." Kris paused for a long moment then finally asked, "Tell me Jack, why do you want to get to know Will Clay?"

It was as though Kris had punched him in the stomach. The blood drained from Jack's face and he was unable to meet Kris's eyes. He finally whispered, "Because he can help me get me what I want."

He felt a hand on his shoulder, and Jack looked up to see that Kris's face was filled with understanding. "Relationship Arrogance is as common as the cold, Jack. But that doesn't stop it from having devastating consequences. When a person is constantly forecasting their return on investment, they become blind to the *person* behind the transaction and this blindness renders them incapable of building real relationships."

Jack sat silently, struggling with the emotions welling up inside of him.

Finally Kris spoke. "Tell me this, Jack. Why am I helping you?"

Before Jack could answer, a billowing gray mist engulfed them. Eventually, the outlines of an adult and several small children appeared and gradually came into focus. Jack realized he was seeing himself lying on his living room floor, wrestling with his pint-sized daughters. He tickled them as they screamed with laughter.

"This was last Sunday," Jack said to Kris. "I was supposed to be getting them ready for bed."

After the giggling stopped, Jack watched himself gather his youngest daughter in his arms.

"Sophy, why do I love you? Is it because of your big blue eyes?" he asked.

"No, Daddy!" the little girl exclaimed. She obviously knew this game.

"No?" Jack said, scratching his head in confusion. "Then I must love you because of how smart you are."

The little girl began to wriggle in delight, shouting out, "No!"

"Oh, now I remember," Jack said. "It's because you are such a good daughter."

"No, that's not why!" she said, falling to the floor in a heap of giggles.

Jack picked her up and set her back on her feet again. "Then why do I love you?" he asked.

"You love me just because I'm me!"

"Right! And what about you, Lynn?" Jack said, pulling another daughter to his side.

"You love me just because I'm me, too, Dad," she said, rolling her eyes but smiling.

"Me too, you love me just because, too!" May and Lauren chimed in.

Laughing, the girls tackled Jack and piled on top of him.

Grace walked in and began scolding them, but was obviously having difficulty maintaining her stern expression. "It is an hour past your bedtime, girls. Kiss your dad good night and get in bed."

As the girls scampered up the stairs, Jack found himself sitting with Kris on a bench back at the mall.

"Why am I helping you?" Kris asked again.

Jack suddenly had a hard time swallowing. "Just because I'm me?"

"Yes. Just because you're you. Building relationships 'just because' is the antidote for Relationship Arrogance. It feels pretty different when someone is getting to know you 'just because,' doesn't it?"

Jack nodded.

"Governors and mayors don't force residents to live inside their cities of influence. People choose to build there because they know the city is governed by someone who genuinely cares about them as a person," Kris said.

He pulled out a key that said *Develop Relationships Just Because* and concluded, "Everyone deserves to be treated that way, including Will Clay."

Jack paused for a moment before finally voicing a question that had been bothering him.

"Are you saying I should never develop a relationship with someone that can help my business?" Jack asked.

Kris threw back his head and laughed until his stomach jiggled.

"Of course not. I'm here to help save your business, not to grab a shovel and throw dirt on the coffin. Governors understand that they will benefit from building strong relationships; the difference is that they don't build those relationships with *specific outcomes* in mind. While they know that opportunities will flow as a result of the newly acquired trust, they haven't predetermined what those look like. They build relationships just because they value people, plain and simple."

"I'm still not quite sure I understand. I mean, I get that Santa Claus does things just because, and I care about my children just because, but translating that into a business relationship…?"

"Can you think of a time where you've built a business relationship *without* a forecasted return on investment?" Kris said. "For example, let's go back to Ted Jacobson at the Kingpin Bowling Alley. Why did you build a relationship with him?"

Jack thought about Ted. "He's just a good guy. I really like him."

"And how did you help his business?"

"I don't remember ever. . ." Jack began, but stopped when he realized what Kris was referring to.

He'd been on an advisory board that put together a corporate sports program, and had lobbied hard to have the bowling tournament at the Kingpin. It wasn't as central as some of the other alleys, but he knew that it would make all the difference to Ted's business, and he finally convinced the others.

"So, you helped Ted 'just because,' and that action came back to serve you in a way you never could've imagined," Kris said.

Jack thought again of Murray and Monty and had to agree.

"Ted didn't give you an immediate transaction, but when he saw an opportunity to help you by making an introduction, he acted. Why? Because you had built a high level of trust with him."

"You make it sound so simple," Jack said.

Kris grasped Jack by the shoulders with his big hands and gave him a penetrating look. "Simple, not easy. Would it have been easy for you to put the needs of David Edwards ahead of your own at lunch the other day?"

Jack sighed, "No."

Kris's smile poured over Jack like a warm shower. "It's more of a process than an event. It's taken me many centuries to perfect, but even though building relationships 'just because' will require effort, I know you can do it. I believe in you."

Jack silently watched as Kris walked back to the sleigh and lifted the first little girl in line onto his lap.

"You look like a ballerina to me," Jack heard him say.

A pleased smile broke over the little girl's face as she nodded.

"Didn't I say you'd like him?" Patrick said, appearing at Jack's side.

"How can you resist someone who likes you 'just because'?" Jack sighed, holding up his hands in defeat.

10.

The Parasite

There'll be white blackbirds before an unwilling woman ties the knot.

—Irish Proverb

As the clock tower above Kris chimed the passing of another hour, Jack found himself back at home, sitting at his desk. He leaned back and closed his eyes as waves of exhaustion began rolling over him. His thoughts began churning through all of his relationships and began dividing themselves into two mental columns: those he'd managed well and those he hadn't. Jack pulled out a piece of paper and created a list of things he needed to do. Writing a thank-you note to Ted Jacobson headed the list.

The whine of an insect broke the silence of the room. It landed on the top of Jack's arm, and he brushed it away. The mosquito shot up and seemed to disappear, but then Jack felt the soft tickle of its legs near his ear. Shaking his head, he heard the whirring of wings as the insect flew away again.

A few seconds later, Jack looked down to see the mosquito perched on his arm, silently siphoning his blood. Jack tried to smash it with his hand, but it escaped. Grabbing a nearby magazine and rolling it up, Jack began chasing the mosquito around the room.

"What seems to be the trouble, lad?"

Jack whirled around.

"Stop it! I swear I'm going to have a heart attack if you keep sneaking up on me like that!" Jack exclaimed.

"My apologies," Patrick said, amused. "What's put a bee in your bonnet?"

"I was just trying to get rid of that stupid mosquito," Jack muttered, still annoyed.

Jack heard a chuckle, and turned to see a broad-shouldered man holding a large cardboard box standing in the doorway. The whiteness of the man's teeth stood out in sharp contrast to his dark skin.

"You know, Jack," the stranger observed, "you and that mosquito actually have a lot in common."

"Why, Chase! Are you finished with your surveillance already?" Patrick asked. He turned to Jack and said, "I'd like you to meet Chase Burrows—a lad with a true talent for uncovering information."

Chase placed the box on the desk, and shook Jack's hand. He then asked for a few minutes to assemble his gear.

As Jack watched him work, he was impressed at the ease with which Chase assembled each piece of equipment. Although he didn't recognize any of the high-tech gadgets, he suspected they weren't available to the average citizen.

"Now," said Chase, as he plugged in the last cable, "let's get down to business. If it's okay, I'm going to start with a couple of questions."

"Shoot," Jack replied.

Folding his arms, Chase leaned back against the wall and said, "I saw your reaction to the mosquito. It seemed to be annoying you."

Jack nodded, embarrassed he'd been caught making a fool of himself.

"Didn't you admire its persistence and tenacity?" Chase asked.

Jack laughed. "No."

Tracking the mosquito as it darted around the room, Chase asked, "Why not?"

"It was distracting me from what I was doing," Jack said, pointing to the half-finished list on his desk. "Not to mention that I now have a bite that is going to swell up and itch."

Chase paused for a moment, drumming his fingers across his mouth. "Like I said, Jack, you and that mosquito have a lot in common. Can you think of a time where your company has behaved like that mosquito?"

Jack was taken aback. What was Chase suggesting?

"Actually, a member of your sales team was a lot like a mosquito two days ago," Chase finally said when Jack didn't respond. "But we'll come back to that in a minute. First, I'd like you to tell me about Will Clay."

"Will Clay is a partner at Clay and Chagall," Jack told him. "We've been trying to recruit their firm as a client. I've heard through the grapevine that they're considering a brand redesign."

"So, your company identified him as someone you wanted to build a relationship with," Chase said. "Then what did you do?"

"We sent him a brochure and a catalogue, and I asked one of my sales directors to follow up."

Jack knew it was an inadequate strategy, but he hadn't been able to come up with any other ideas. What was he supposed to do? Storm the offices of Clay & Chagall and demand their brand join the twenty-first century?

"Well, let's see how your efforts have fared so far."

Chase pulled out several pieces of crumpled paper from the cardboard box, smoothing them out on the desk in front of Jack. "This is a letter your staff mailed to Will. Take note of the format." Chase pointed to various parts of the letter as he spoke, running his finger down the line of copy. "You assume right here that he's unhappy with their current brand, then you talk about how Dillon-Parker can guarantee the lowest price. Finally, you say you will call to arrange a time to meet with him. I retrieved this from the trash, by the way."

Jack felt his face go red.

"But that's the way you build new accounts, Chase," Jack said, picking up the sales literature and examining it with a critical eye. "Everyone does it like this. It's a numbers game. I tell my people to be persistent and keep working the account until the client breaks down and lets you come in for a sales call. We've been trying for weeks, and the other day one of my agents said he finally had a conversation with Will."

"Yes, he did," Chase responded. He pushed a red button on one of the gadgets. "Let's go ahead and replay that memorable moment."

A recorded conversation between a man and a woman began to play.

Woman:	This will adversely affect our earnings next quarter. (knock at the door)
Man:	Sorry, Will, but that guy from Dillon-Parker is on the phone again. He insists on speaking with you. Should I say you aren't available?
Will:	(pause) When is this guy going to quit? No, I'll take the call. Sorry Anne, this will only take a minute. I guess some people just have to take it the hard way.

Splat!

Jack jumped. He turned to see Patrick, a fly swatter in hand, standing over the splattered remains of an insect on the desk in front of him.

"Pay your last respects to the mosquito," Patrick announced.

Jack sat silently for a moment, depressed. "Great," he muttered under his breath.

Chase looked at him steadily. "Jack, you have an important decision to make here. You can either tell yourself Will Clay is a jerk and that you didn't do anything wrong, or you can face the truth about the inept way your organization tries to build relationships."

Several different expressions flitted across Jack's face—stubbornness, pride, and embarrassment.

"Well, I'd rather not be a smashed bug," he finally said. He stood up and swept the incriminating evidence into the wastebasket. "It seems my relationship system could be more effective. Any suggestions?"

"Well, for starters, you need to replace your outdated gladiator techniques with the relationship systems of a governor," Chase explained.

He asked if he could use Jack's computer, and was soon logging into what looked like an online encyclopedia.

Pulling up a page labeled "Parasites and Pollinators," he asked Jack to read it out loud.

Jack cleared his throat and read, "In nature, life forms can exist in either a symbiotic or a parasitic fashion. Diagram 4a depicts the Culex pipiens, commonly known as the household mosquito. It extracts what it needs from its current host and then moves on to find a new host—textbook parasitic behavior."

At this point, Chase stopped him and said, "I call this method the dine and ditch. Parasites persistently go after a relationship until they get what they want and then suddenly disappear."

Jack winced at how accurately this described many of his business relationships.

"So how does a governor do it?" he asked.

Chase pointed to the second diagram on the screen and began reading where Jack had left off.

"Diagram 4b shows an Apis mellifera, or honey bee," Chase read. "The bee also extracts the nectar it needs, but leaves behind something that insures the flower's survival."

"Pollen," Jack broke in.

"Right. The bee actively contributes to the flower's survival through the pollen it leaves behind," Chase explained. "Governors are pollinators. Instead of living like the mosquito, always on the hunt for the next transaction without any regard for the long-term relationship, they always leave behind as much or more than they take."

So it isn't wrong to get what you need, Jack thought. *You just need to give back.*

Chase pointed back to the flower in the diagram, as he concluded, "The paradox is that by ensuring the success of others, pollinators also guarantee their own."

Chase explained the parasite-pollinator principle wasn't a key—but that it provided the groundwork for the next key Jack would receive.

"That key outlines the relationship process used by pollinators," he said, "a process that will help you build a relationship with anyone."

"Anyone but Will Clay," Jack said dejectedly. "If he already sees us as parasites, that relationship is probably a lost cause."

"I wouldn't worry about that," Chase replied. "Right before I left, I received approval from headquarters to delete that phone call. As of this moment, it never happened."

Patrick let out a low whistle. "You got permission to change the past? I'll wager you had a time getting that approved."

"I had to pull a few strings but after I saw Jack's footage, I felt that desperate times called for desperate measures." Chase turned to Jack and said, "I just wanted you to know what it feels like to be a governor instead of a bloodthirsty parasite."

11

Learn, Serve, Grow

When the apple is ripe, it will fall.

—Irish Proverb

"You're looking a bit haggard, lad," Patrick said, a note of concern in his voice. "We've a few minutes to spare. Why don't you take a small break."

Jack nodded gratefully and headed for the bathroom. Flipping on the light, he examined himself in the mirror.

"You look like you've been hit by a truck," he told his reflection.

His hair was matted down, sticking out in odd places, and dark circles had formed underneath his eyes. Jack knew these signs of exhaustion weren't the result of tonight's adventures; he'd been burning the candle on both ends for almost a year now, and it was starting to show.

He turned the silver handle of the faucet and held a washcloth under the stream of cold water. As he rubbed the cloth over his face, he heard the muffled clanging of the clock in the hall.

He lowered the cloth and looked at the mirror, then let out a startled yelp, and stumbled backward. As he fell he tipped over the large garbage can that had appeared behind him. Wadded-up paper towels and pieces of chewing gum spilled out across the tile floor of a public bathroom.

Jack straightened himself and scrambled back to the mirror. Running his fingers over his face in awe, he stared at a much younger version of himself. Not only had the dark circles disappeared, but the fine lines that had formed over the last ten years had vanished as well.

Behind him, a short young man with carrot-red hair entered the bathroom and approached the sink next to Jack.

"Top of the morning to you, lad," he said, as he filled his hands with soap from the dispenser. "You're the spitting image of your great-uncle Calvin at this age."

"Patrick? Is that you?" Jack's gaze jerked away from his own reflection to stare at the boy beside him. "You look like you're twelve."

Patrick lifted up his chin, clearly offended. "I'm nearly sixteen, and I took enough bashing from the lads down in the village about my size, so there's no need for you to be adding your two bits."

Patrick dried his hands and motioned for Jack to follow him.

"Where are we going?" Jack asked nervously, suddenly seized with the fear that he might have to relive his formative years.

"'Tis a fine day for a ramble down memory lane," Patrick said, holding open the bathroom door for Jack.

Seeing no alternative, Jack followed Patrick out into a large hallway lined with lockers and classrooms.

"Oak Grove High," Jack muttered, looking around in awe. "I'm back in high school!"

As he walked down the hall, Jack began experiencing some benefits from this plunge back into his youth. Every step seemed to increase his energy and his adult troubles began melting away. Even his perpetual tension headache had disappeared.

The bell rang, releasing rush hour. Every inch of the hallway was suddenly filled with teenagers. Jack began pointing out different people to Patrick as they walked down the hall.

"Do you see that girl across the hall, over in the corner?" Jack asked.

Patrick looked over to where a vivacious brunette with a mouthful of braces stood, surrounded by a group of friends.

"You mean the one talking and talking?" Patrick asked, after he'd observed her for a moment in amazement. "Does she ever come up for air?"

"Nope, it's my little sister Amy, and oxygen only slows her down."

"Well, there's an Irish proverb that says, 'whenever there are women, there's talking and whenever there's geese, there's cackling,'" Patrick replied with a wink.

Jack stopped as if by instinct at his old locker and began twisting the dial to see if he could remember his combination.

"Hey, Green Machine!" a voice from behind him called out.

Instantly responding to his old nickname, Jack turned around to see Mark Child, his best friend from high school, standing in front of him. Automatically, he put his hand out to perform their signature handshake.

"Mark! It's so good to see you!" Jack exclaimed.

Shooting him a look that plainly asked whether he'd lost his mind, Mark responded, "Yeah . . . it's good to see you, too. That whole class period away from you was rough."

Then his face suddenly cracked into a grin, and he threw an arm around Jack's shoulder, playfully jabbing him in the ribs. "I'm just giving you a hard time, man. Hopefully next time I won't have to go to these kinds of extremes to spend some time with you."

Jack stopped dead and looked over at Mark. "Wait a second," he said. "Are you telling me that *you're* my next trainer?"

"A rookie, true, but fully certified; I completed the training a couple of years ago." Mark told him. "When the Foundation asked me where I wanted to hold my session of your training, I couldn't think of a better place then good ol' Oak Grove High."

Looking back and forth between Mark and Patrick, a suspicion suddenly sprouted inside Jack's brain. "You didn't have anything to do with me being er . . . *selected* for this training, did you, Mark?"

"What are friends for?" he replied with a wicked grin. "C'mon let's get going."

"Where are we going?" Jack asked.

"Well, technically you're supposed to be in English reciting 'The Road Less Traveled,' but somehow I don't think you're up to that today, so let's go to first lunch instead."

"I'll be leaving you to it," Patrick said, and disappeared into the crowd of students.

Mark and Jack walked into the huge commons area at the center of the school, and they saw teenagers of all shapes and sizes lounging on the carpeted risers or standing in tight clusters along the walls. The area was divided into the well-defined territories of the athletes, the brains, the rebels, and the drama and music crowds.

"Look at us," Jack said, taking a seat on a riser that had a panoramic view of the entire commons. "It's like we thought we'd come down with an infectious disease if we talked to someone we didn't know."

"We were all pretty insecure, that's for sure," Mark agreed, as he lounged back on his elbows beside Jack. "So, how's the training been so far?" he asked curiously.

"Pretty good, actually. I'm starting to understand why it's important to build relationships and what my objectives should be," Jack said. "But I'm still a little hazy on how I consciously go out and do it. Don't relationships just happen?"

"Sure," Mark replied, "but understanding how relationships naturally develop can help you to build them intentionally."

Mark stopped and seemed to make up his mind about something.

"At this point, I could just walk you through the process of building a relationship, but I think it'll make more sense if you experience it firsthand."

Behind them, there was a sudden commotion, and Jack turned to see four large boys herding a smaller boy around the corner.

"Hey, that looks like . . ." Jack turned back to Mark, his eyebrows shooting up. "You chose that day, huh?"

Mark nodded affirmatively.

"I'll be right back," Jack told him.

Jack sprinted down the hallway and around a corner. As he rounded the bend, he saw a pair of legs sticking out of a garbage can. He broke through the pack that surrounded the garbage can, and placed himself between it and the bullies.

"Do you know why my friends call me the Green Machine?" he asked, nose-to-nose with the largest boy.

"No. Why don't you tell us," the boy replied jeeringly, trying unsuccessfully to match Jack's intensity.

"It's because I can rip a bully like you apart in about thirty seconds. Believe me, I'm not somebody you want to mess with."

The boy breathed heavily through his nose, sizing Jack up. Then he broke eye contact and turned back to his friends. "C'mon, let's go. This guy's a freak."

Jack turned to find the boy had extricated himself from the garbage can and was cleaning off his thick glasses with the edge of his shirt.

"You all right?" Jack asked

"Yeah, I guess," the boy muttered, but when he saw Jack's expression he added, "Don't worry, this is a pretty normal first day. I should be used to it by now."

He looked down and kicked the floor in frustration.

"Let's get out of here," Jack said, jerking his chin in the direction of the commons.

As they walked down the hallway, the boy asked, "So, what's your name?"

"What? Oh. . . I'm Jack. Jack Green."

"I'm Darrin Clark," the boy said. "I just transferred here from Austin, but I'm not from there either. I'm not from anywhere, really. My dad works for the military, so we move around a lot."

As they neared the commons, Darrin's body became more and more translucent until he eventually disappeared altogether. Jack looked around and saw Mark waving him over.

"I haven't talked to Darrin in years. Have you heard from him lately?" Jack asked as he sat down.

"Actually, I talked to him last week. He and his wife just moved, and I called to get their new address. As we were talking about old times, your Superman heroics came up, and I realized I'd never asked you why you did it."

"Well, back before you knew me, I was a pretty chubby kid and dealt with more than my fair share of bullies," Jack explained, staring down the group of offending boys as they slunk back into the commons area. "Ever since then, I've had zero tolerance for the creeps."

"How you developed your friendship with Darrin is the same way you'd build one with anyone else, so let's analyze it. How did Darrin transition from being 'the kid in the dumpster' to one of your best friends?"

Unzipping his backpack, Mark took out a marker, and grabbed a banner from a pile of discarded dance decorations. He wrote on the back of it:

Learn: To come to understand.

"Learning is the beginning stage of all relationships—learning what people like, don't like, or how they think and feel. It's especially important during this stage to try to understand the other person's wants and needs," Mark explained. "So what kinds of things did you learn about Darrin that first day?"

Jack immediately thought about what Darrin had said to him in the hallway.

"I learned that his dad was in the military and he'd never stayed in the same school for more than a couple of years. Because of that, making friends didn't come easily to him. Oh, and of course it only took a few hours of hanging out with him to discover his addiction to soda," Jack said, ticking off the different pieces of information on his fingers as he listed them.

Recalling the first time he'd seen his new friend's bedroom, Jack remembered the national awards from chess and debate tournaments that had covered every inch of wall space, giving Jack his first clue that his new friend was a master strategist.

"Good," Mark said when Jack mentioned this, "but you're still missing something. As we got to know Darrin better, we heard more than we ever wanted to hear about something that was *really* important to him."

Mark pointed to where a petite blonde sat eating her lunch with the tennis team.

"Melanie Harris," Jack said and slowly began to grin. "How could I forget? He was the brain and she was the athlete, and the whole thing being completely hopeless just seemed to make him like her more."

"As you learn about people, you'll eventually stumble across specific wants or needs they have, like you did with Darrin. This is critical because identifying what someone needs then helping them get it will build a relationship faster than anything else."

Mark uncapped the lid of another marker and wrote "serve" in big letters below "learn."

Serve: To be of assistance to or promote the interests of.

"So, how did you help him with Melanie?"

"Wait a second, that was a group effort," Jack protested. "I may have brought the issue to everyone's attention, but if I remember, inviting her to an all-night Risk tournament and putting her on Darrin's team was your idea."

"I'll never forget them crushing the rest of us into a bloody pulp as they ruthlessly conquered the world," Mark added reminiscently.

"End result: they dated their senior year. Mission accomplished," Jack said, wiping his hands in satisfaction over a job well done.

Mark added that although helping other people to achieve specific wants and needs was often the fastest way to build a relationship, there were other ways to serve as well. Being genuinely interested in what people had to say, spending time with them doing what they liked to do, or remembering important events—all were "serves" because each of these actions built higher levels of trust.

Mark then wrote "grow" underneath the words "learn" and "serve."

Grow: To have an increasing influence.

"Can you think of opportunities that came to you because of your friendship with Darrin?" Mark asked.

"Yeah, when I ran for student body president," he said. "The rest of you were good for a few laughs, but it was Darrin who got me elected."

Jack remembered how Darrin had transformed his bedroom into campaign headquarters. It looked like he was planning a full military coup by the way it was decked out with graphs, charts, and slogans.

"His dad was pretty high up in the military," Jack recalled. "But I still don't know how he was able to swing getting us a tank. I'll never forget the day he parked it on the high school patio completely covered with banners that said 'Vote for the Green Machine.'"

"The other candidates didn't stand a chance," Mark said, shaking his head.

"Nope, it was shock and awe from beginning to end," Jack agreed, grinning as he remembered the crowds of kids swarming around the tank at lunch hour. "Darrin also spent hours coaching me on my speech. It was his idea to give it like a drill sergeant."

"That speech became an Oak Grove High legend," Mark agreed.

Jack could still see himself on the stage, bellowing out orders to the student body. It had been one of the most memorable moments of his life, and he had Darrin to thank for it.

"But we were friends," Jack said, suddenly realizing what Mark was getting at. "I didn't build a relationship with him so I could win an election, and I would've still been his friend even if he hadn't helped me."

"Relax. We're dissecting a natural phenomenon here," Mark explained. "When you effectively learn about people and serve them 'just because,' they naturally *want* to reciprocate and help you accomplish your goals as well. That's just how the 'grow' part of the cycle works."

Jack hadn't really thought of it that way. The end result of learning and serving was that people just wanted to help you, even if that wasn't your intent in building the relationship in the first place?

Mark held out a key that had *Learn, Serve, Grow* engraved on it and said, "The Learn, Serve, Grow cycle describes the process of building sustainable relationships. As you continue to learn and serve 'just because' you will gain greater access to each other's time, influence, and resources. But remember it's a cycle, and just like any other cycle, it needs to be repeated over and over again to keep the relationship strong."

Jack looked down at the key thoughtfully. Learn, Serve, Grow. It seemed fairly straightforward and uncomplicated.

Mark looked out into the sea of faces in the commons and pointed out a pretty dark-haired girl who was flirting with one of the basketball players.

"If I remember, Stacy Reynolds was your favorite subject in high school. I'll never forget the day you finally got up the courage to ask her to the Homecoming dance."

A flood of memories washed over Jack. Stacy Reynolds! She hadn't crossed his mind in years, yet in high school she'd been all he could think about. Midterms, gym class, and homework he could do without, but he suddenly missed the rush of wondering if a girl would ever give him the time of day.

"Yeah, I waited my entire high school career to go out with her, and when she was finally my girlfriend, everything fell apart." Jack still remembered his frustration at the situation. "She made me cookies, left me notes, and would call me, but whenever I tried to do things for her, I could see her get worried, like I was going to think she was a burden or something. It got so one-sided that I finally had to end it."

"She didn't understand the Law of Grow," Mark said.

He scribbled something on the banner and handed it to Jack.

Law of Grow: Relationships are strongest when balanced. Continually learning and serving without allowing the other person the same opportunity will weaken the relationship over time.

"Making continual demands on a relationship will weaken it, but so will never allowing the other person to reciprocate. It's a delicate balance," Mark said.

"I'll just stick this banner in Stacy's locker; I'm sure she'll appreciate it," Jack responded with a smile.

Mark reached inside his backpack again, and this time he pulled out the relationship wish list Jack had created with Cordelia.

"Here's the list of relationships you wanted to work on this year," Mark said, looking over Jack's shoulder as he read through the list of names. "What's your plan?"

"I guess the first thing I need to do is learn about these people and find out about their needs," Jack replied. "Then when I get the chance, I need to try and serve those needs."

"Right," Mark said, "but always remember that although Learn, Serve, Grow is a process, that doesn't mean it's an equation that produces a predictable result." Mark pointed through the window to where different trees, bushes, and flowers edged the sides of the patio. "Governors see relationships as seeds that they plant and nurture, but they understand that it's not until after the plant matures that they will find out whether they planted a vegetable, a flower, or a tree. It's important to remember the Learn, Serve, Grow cycle is designed to help you form a *relationship*—not a specific outcome."

12.

Pools

Listen to the sound of the river and you will get a trout.

—Irish Proverb

A bell rang and students flooded through the hallways headed for their next class. As Jack watched, the scene slowly began to blur like a camera going out of focus. Then, feeling like he was waking from a long and restful sleep, Jack opened his eyes to find himself sitting next to Patrick, floating down a river in a large wooden rowboat.

As he tried to get his bearings, Jack saw a woman materialize in front of him. She looked as surprised as he did, but when she caught sight of Patrick, she shrieked with delight. The giant hug she gave him nearly capsized the boat.

"Patrick!" she exclaimed as she released him. "I am so glad to see you! I haven't been able to concentrate on anything since I got your message."

Patrick took the woman's hands in his and looked her over.

"Maggie, my darling! Look at you shined up like a penny!" he exclaimed.

Maggie glanced down at her fishing vest and chuckled appreciatively. "Still spouting the blarney, I see." She then turned to Jack. "And you must be Jack. I imagine you're wondering which way is up these days."

"That way, right?" Jack said, pointing to the river.

"Exactly!" Maggie replied, trying to suppress a smile. "For weeks after my training I was positively paranoid another 'expert' was going to pop up, armed with my next lesson." She rolled her large blue eyes. "And look at me now. I'm one of them!"

"Do you work for Fish Village?" Jack asked, noticing the resort's name on the cap she wore.

Fish Village had been nicknamed the "Fisherman's Mecca," because of its reputation for drawing fishermen from all parts of the globe. Jack had friends who'd recently stayed there and couldn't stop talking about it.

Patrick looked amused. "Maggie's the proprietress, lad."

Maggie smiled, a little embarrassed, but affirmed that she was indeed the owner.

"It isn't something I've always been proud of," she admitted. "There was a time, right before I met Patrick, that I would've given Fish Village to anyone who would've taken it. And good riddance to it, as far as I was concerned, so long as I could walk away and never look back."

"I can relate," Jack said, thinking of all the times he'd considered putting Dillon-Parker on the auction block.

The soft breeze sent a shiver through the aspen trees that lined the bank and seemed to carry Jack's dark thoughts away with it. The rushing sound of the river and the warm wood against his skin made him feel strangely relaxed, like a cat basking in the sunlight.

"I think I'm going to like this field trip," he announced.

"'Tis a fine day, to be sure, but the lesson isn't up here. It's down there," Patrick said, pointing into the river.

Under the reflection of the trees and mountains, Jack saw flashes of movement in the water. "Look at those fish," Jack exclaimed as he moved to his knees to get a closer look. "They're huge!"

The water rippled and flowed over the fish, prisms of color flashing out as their silver scales caught the sunlight.

Maneuvering herself to sit beside Jack, Maggie asked, "What do you notice about the way they are positioning themselves in the water?"

"They're all facing upstream." There was a note of surprise in Jack's voice as he said this. "I always thought fish swam downstream with the current, but they're keeping a steady position."

Patrick nodded. "Their survival depends on what they can catch floating downstream, but fighting the current 'tis bitter hard work and a fish can be standing it for only so long."

"It looks effortless from here," Jack said, still studying the fish.

"Let me show you a few of our best fishing spots," Maggie suggested.

She grabbed the paddles and began rowing downstream, her capable hands pulling the oars through the water as though she had been born doing it. Navigating the boat toward a stretch of water tinged with a subtle green hue, she brought the boat alongside the trunk of a fallen tree.

"Listen, Jack. What do you hear?"

Jack listened. "It's quiet. You can barely hear the current."

Looking down into the still water, he saw it was teaming with fish.

"There are pockets like this all along the river," Maggie explained. "They're created when something— a rock, a tree, or a bend in the river— slows the flow of the current. When a fish needs a break from fighting the current, it will seek shelter in a pool like this one."

She slowly navigated the boat around the outside edge of the pool and pointed out a large fish whose scales bulged around its belly. "For instance, do you see that fat trout in the middle? For the last three weeks that crazy guy has been swimming in this pool at exactly the same place and time."

"Don't get me wrong, this is really interesting, but what does it have to do with building relationships?" Jack asked, confused.

Jack's stomach suddenly dropped like he'd just blasted off in a rocket. The next thing he knew, he was standing on the ledge of a skyscraper watching as the river below him transformed into a city street crammed with rush-hour traffic. Looking down the 100-story drop, Jack's knees buckled and he pitched forward. Two pairs of hands shot out and pulled him backward. Maggie and Patrick guided Jack off the ledge and onto the roof, hovering over him anxiously.

"Just a 'wee' bit of warning, that's all I ask," Jack said, lifting his head to glare at Patrick.

"I beg your pardon, lad. We didn't mean to give you a start," Patrick said, sounding contrite.

Patrick waited until Jack's breathing evened out before asking him if he was ready to continue. Jack nodded and stood up.

"Well, then, I'd like you to look over this fair city and tell me what you see," Patrick said.

Jack inched his way over to the ledge and gazed at the scene below. "It's New York. I can tell by the skyline. There's Brooklyn Bridge," he said, pointing out the familiar structure. He observed the people rushing along the sidewalks and across the street. "It looks like everyone's heading for work."

"Now, think back to the river . . . do you see any similarities?" Maggie asked.

As Jack looked out over the city again, the scene morphed before his eyes. The street wound and twisted like the river, a dull roar rising from it like the sound of white water rapids. The yellow, silver, and blue cars transformed into fish, moving in and out of the current, fighting for survival. The people on the sidewalks and those filling the offices in the adjacent buildings transformed into fish, locked in the struggle to get ahead the best they could.

"I get it," Jack said slowly. "The current . . . and the fish."

"Do you be seeing how the speed of the current keeps them separated?" Patrick asked.

Jack nodded. The scenario was all too familiar.

"Just like fish, business leaders spend the majority of their day fighting for survival in the current," Maggie explained, her gaze sweeping over the congested streets, crowded sidewalks, and office buildings below them.

"In business, the current represents task-oriented, results-driven work environments where production and efficiency are the primary drivers."

That about sums up my entire life, Jack thought

"Regardless of whether you work in a high-rise in Manhattan or in a regional business like Dillon-Parker," Maggie continued, "people tend to spend the majority of their time in the current doing the 'work' of their business. They're selling, marketing, ordering, managing staff, paying the bills, and juggling a million other things."

Maggie pointed to the building across the way. Jack could see people hurrying between the cubicles with bulging files in their hands. Others were either talking on their phones or glued to their computer screens, typing furiously.

"Can you see how difficult it would be to build a relationship with people when they are inside the current?" Maggie asked. "Interrupt people when they are entrenched in their task-driven mindset, and they're sure to see you as a parasite or even worse. In contrast, a correctly designed pool is the perfect environment for relationship building."

As Jack remembered the fish he'd seen swimming lazily through the pool, he suddenly realized he couldn't remember the last time he'd really relaxed and connected with others in a professional setting.

"Pools are events or places that remove a person from their 'work mindset' and reconnect them with the people surrounding them," Maggie said. "People who wouldn't give you the time of day while in the current, quickly transform inside the relaxed pace of a pool."

The street slowly took on a bluish hue as the scene began to shift. Jack tried to grab onto the ledge, but it evaporated beneath his fingers and he dropped through space again. Frantically trying to break his fall, he reached out and caught something solid. Curling his fingers around it, he opened his eyes and found himself clutching the side of the boat.

"They've got to build something like this at an amusement park," Jack said breathlessly, his heart still thudding against his ribs. "It would make millions."

"We try to keep you on your toes," Patrick replied with a modest shrug of his shoulders.

Maggie unzipped a pocket of her fishing vest and took out a set of keys.

"Pools are the 'where' of relationship-building and are the best places to begin the Learn, Serve, Grow cycle," Maggie said as she selected a gold key and held it out to Jack. Engraved on it were the words *Swim in Pools.*

Patrick then nudged Jack and pointed to the surface of the water. "Take a gander at that wee little fish. What a sad fellow he is."

Handing the key back to Maggie, Jack looked down into the water to see a silver fish straining desperately against the current. It gradually slowed down, out of what appeared to be pure exhaustion, and was carried downstream several feet. While trying to maintain its position, the fish kept his mouth wide open, darting to catch anything coming down the river.

Jack felt a sudden rush of pity for the fish. "That fish is pretty hard-core. Why doesn't he swim into that pool?" he said, pointing to where several large gray boulders had slowed the current. "He's never going to survive at this rate."

"His name is Jack Green," Maggie replied. "He works fourteen-hour days, then heads home to his family pool, eats and sleeps, and plunges back into the current again."

Jack stared down at the fish. He felt a prickle run down the back of his neck as he noticed an odd resemblance.

"We're not saying you shouldn't be spending time in the current doing the work of your business," Patrick continued, before Jack could protest, "but to build influence you must swim in pools as well."

The little silver fish continued to swim frantically against the current, but was swept further and further downstream.

"I do feel like that fish most of the time," Jack admitted. "It seems the harder I fight, the further I get behind."

13

Fish Village

May the holes in your net be no larger than the fish in it.

—Irish Proverb

They quietly watched the fish until it finally disappeared from view. A bird call broke the silence, its song echoing off the jagged mountain cliffs. Maggie then reached into one of her pockets and pulled out a laminated card in the shape of a fish.

"As important as being out of the current is," she said, "it's only one of the many ingredients needed to build an effective pool."

She handed Jack the card:

```
Pools

1. Outside the Current

2. Effective Pull

3. Connects the Participants

4. Duplicable

5. Name

6. Culture
```

Maggie pointed to the second ingredient. "For a pool to be effective, it not only has to be outside the current, but it also must have enough 'pull' to draw people in. The fish have to *want* to come."

"True. I'm invited to events all the time, but I only go to the ones that sound exciting," Jack agreed.

"People intuitively understand that a pool must have the first two ingredients," Maggie told him. "It's the third ingredient that is often overlooked—which really is a shame because facilitating interaction between the participants is the whole point of a pool."

Maggie asked Jack if he'd ever attended an event that was outside the current and had effective pull, but where he hadn't built any new relationships. An example instantly popped into his mind. He described a conference he'd recently attended with dynamic speakers and relevant topics, but the participants had been herded from one venue to the next without any opportunity to interact. Jack didn't connect with a single person during the entire two-day event.

"And yet, they could've taken that experience from average to exceptional simply by facilitating some relationship-building," Maggie said, shaking her head.

Remembering how isolated he'd felt during the conference, Jack had to agree with her.

"The fourth ingredient is making the pool duplicable," Maggie continued. "What would be the advantage of designing a pool that could be held more than once?"

Jack gazed meditatively over the river.

"Relationships need time to develop," he finally said. "Interacting with a person one time isn't going to build a very strong relationship. Plus it may take a couple of times in the same pool before I trust that the experience will be worth my time."

"We have a saying in Ireland: the mason who strikes often is better than the one who strikes too hard," Patrick added.

"Have you noticed how he seems to have a proverb for every situation?" Maggie asked, completely breaking away from the subject. "I've been wondering for years if they're real or if he just makes them up."

"Aye, now that be a trade secret, lass," Patrick replied with a wink. "And you'd best be hurrying because we're coming up on the dock."

"The last two ingredients are to give your pool a name and to create its culture," Maggie concluded. "Patrick, these are two of your favorites, why don't you take it from here?"

"I'd be pleased to!" Patrick responded. "You see, Jack, most lads and lasses will spend loads of time creating the perfect pool, then, like they have heads full of cider, select its name as an afterthought. It destroys the craft not to learn it properly!"

Patrick became so passionate, that, for a second time, the boat nearly capsized. He apologized as he helped steady the boat, but carried on with his point. "Answer me this. Have you ever decided not to attend a luncheon, forum, convention or, saints forbid, a lecture?"

"Of course. That is, unless I needed a good nap," Jack replied dryly.

"Do you see how naming the pool plays a part in making it effective?" Patrick asked. "And carefully crafting your culture is even more important. True pool builders are masters at packaging their pools so even the most contrary lads and lasses are looking forward to swimming in them."

"You *create* a culture?" Jack asked.

"Designed emotion is one of the secrets of true pool-builders," Patrick responded. "If you're after bringing people back, you must first decide on the mood you want to create, then build an environment fostering those emotions," Patrick explained. "If you're wanting to create a culture of excitement and energy, you'll take a different tack than you would if you're wanting them to feel calm and reflective. It's not the event itself that creates the desire to return, it's the memory of the emotion."

Jack thought back to the places he loved to be. Whether it was at the football stadium or the long stretch of beach where his family often spent their Saturday afternoons, he agreed that it was the *feelings* these places created that drew him back again.

Maggie guided the boat to a large inlet in the river, and around the bend they saw a bustling pier with all shapes and sizes of boats docked alongside it.

Above the pier, nestled among a forest of pines and aspens, stood an enormous, rough-hewn lodge. The words *Fish Village* were engraved on the center of the rock wall in front of the lodge, and a waterfall cascaded over the bronze fish sculptures in the pool beneath. Jack drew in his breath; he hadn't realized he might get the chance to visit the luxurious resort.

Maggie guided the boat toward the dock and then jumped out to secure the boat to a pillar using a stout gray rope.

"I guess this is good-bye," she said, obviously reluctant to leave. "I need to take care of the finishing touches for our annual Fattest Fish Competition. It's our largest pool of the year, and if I don't get back soon, my staff will probably throw me in the river! But, I'll be seeing you both again soon enough," she finished, brightening at the thought.

"Thank you, Maggie," Jack said. "For everything."

"It was my pleasure," Maggie replied. Then she added in a confidential whisper, "For future reference, it's much more fun being on this side of the training."

She waved good-bye and was soon swallowed up by the thick pine trees lining the path. Patrick and Jack climbed out of the boat and sat on the long wooden dock, enjoying the sunshine.

Gazing down the river's sparkling snakelike path, Jack noticed a slackening in the current and traced it back to its source: a large mound of sticks and mud. A beaver suddenly appeared on the top of the dam carrying a stick between its teeth, its fur matted down with water.

"Look! A beaver," Jack said, pointing it out to Patrick. "It always amazes me how animals can build things like that."

He watched the beaver drop the stick on the mound, then creep down the outside of the dam and plunge back into the river.

"If you think that's a sight to be seen, follow me and I'll show you an even bigger one."

Patrick led Jack up the trail, and within moments they were standing inside the front lobby of Fish Village. Jack's attention was immediately drawn to two large photographs that had been carefully hung above the stone fireplace. One picture showed two men proudly holding up a prize trout. The other picture captured three guests sprawled out on the bank of the river, their poles hanging over the water and their hats pulled over their eyes.

Jack and Patrick passed by the Fish Village restaurant, spa, and indoor convention space before stepping out onto a balcony that overlooked the enormous patio that skirted the backside of the lodge. Below them were dozens of people dressed in hats and fishing vests. The place felt alive with energy as groups of people talked and broke into laughter. The smell of fresh salmon sizzling on the grill made Jack's mouth water.

Maggie stood up in front and quieted the group. "Welcome to Fish Village's Annual Fattest Fish Competition."

She explained that the competition would begin soon and that each team was required to report back with their catches no later than eight o'clock that night.

"As you all know, the person who brings in the fattest fish wins a weekend stay at Fish Village and a $5,000 shopping spree at the store."

There was clapping and catcalling from the audience; their enthusiasm was infectious.

"But before I turn you loose," Maggie continued, "let's take some time to get to know each other. You all know the drill. During the first minute, talk about your best fishing experience and during the second minute share a little bit about your professional life."

Maggie rang an old cowbell, and one person at each table began talking while the others listened.

"This is her pool?" Jack asked, impressed.

Patrick nodded. He explained Maggie had realized it would be impossible for her to attend all the pools her key relationships swam in. So, she'd decided to invite them to join her at Fish Village instead.

"When the available pools aren't meeting a governors' needs, they must think like a beaver and create their own," Patrick said.

Jack thought back to Maggie's criteria. The resort was outside the business current, and this event obviously had enough pull. It also had a name and a culture, and she'd mentioned it was an annual event, so it must be duplicable.

Jack shared these observations with Patrick, ticking off each ingredient as he did so. "Wait, I'm forgetting one," he said, pulling out his card to check himself. "Connect the participants!"

Patrick nodded. "Aye. Did you notice how Maggie facilitated interaction to help the participants build their influence? When you structure an event that connects people with relationships they care about, they'll always come back to swim again."

14.

Levels of Relationship

By degrees the castles are built.

—Irish Proverb

Jack found himself sitting at his desk again, the chimes from the hallway clock signaling the passing of another hour. As they faded, he could hear the soft patter of raindrops falling on the slate roof of his house. Going to the window, Jack nudged it open and inhaled deeply.

"Okay, so the answer is building my city of influence," he murmured to himself, so absorbed in his thoughts that he barely registered the loud crack of thunder that broke right over the house. "But where do I start?"

He clenched the window ledge in frustration, feeling as though he were living thousands of years ago watching lightning strike for the first time. He could see the power, but he didn't know how to harness it.

A bolt of lightning lit up the dark street. Jack thought he saw the outline of a man scurrying up the walkway, but when another flash illuminated the landscape, no one was there.

"*Ja*, you need a formula!" a voice boomed out behind him.

Jack's heart jumped. He whirled around to see a pair of wire-rimmed glasses suspended in midair. Gradually a thatch of salt-and-pepper hair, a deeply lined face, and a wiry body wearing a lab coat filled in the empty spaces.

After he finished arriving, the man came forward and shook Jack's hand. "*Guten Tag*. I am Professor Milo Schwartz," he said. Then, noticing Jack's expression, he added, "It seems I have alarmed you. For this I am sorry."

"I guess I should be used to it by now," Jack responded, shaking his head.

Pulling a small black notebook from the pocket of his lab coat, Milo turned his piercing blue eyes on Jack.

"Forgive me. I will need time to gather data," he said.

Milo drew Jack away from the window and circled around him, rising up on his tiptoes and bending down as if making mental notes on every inch of his body. He then began firing off questions about Jack's background and interests, scribbling down notes as he listened to his answers.

"You say that you ran track in high school?" Milo asked checking his notes.

"Yes, I ran the 100-meter dash."

"Tell me, what was your time when you began?"

"It was around fourteen seconds, I think." Jack pictured himself in his first track uniform, gasping for air as he tried to keep up with the rest of the team. He'd worked hard for every second he'd shaved off his time.

"Why was it the coach timed you?" Milo asked, tapping his pen against the flat of his palm.

"So I could know how fast I was," Jack replied, wondering where this was leading. "Once I knew where I was, I could begin improving my time."

"That is right!" Milo boomed out. "Without measurement you cannot see progression. It is the same with relationships; to increase the quality, you must measure your current level of influence."

Milo closed his notebook and asked if he could use the adjoining room. Jack agreed and as he opened the door for the professor, he discovered two large boxes already sitting on the floor. The two men went into the storage room and began unpacking the boxes, lifting out twisted tubes, glass beakers, and other equipment. Within minutes the room was transformed into a small laboratory.

Milo pulled on a pair of plastic gloves and began pouring various liquids and powders into the beakers, creating bright hues of canary yellow and turquoise. Muttering to himself in German, he placed the beakers over two portable burners and soon the liquid began to pucker and finally bubble.

The fax machine on Jack's desk suddenly powered up and began spitting out a list of names.

Jack's eyebrows shot up in surprise. "Who would fax me at this time of night?"

"Ah! For me, I think," Milo explained, going to the machine and picking up the sheaf of papers. "*Ja*, it is a listing of the people inside your city of influence. We can now measure your city's population and quality index."

"Quality index?" Jack asked curiously.

Milo explained that every person inside Jack's city of influence had a quality level assigned to them based on the strength of the relationship.

"Increasing your city's population is important, but you must not forget to increase the quality of your relationships as well."

There was a loud popping sound from one of the beakers, and Milo hurried over to the glass container. He picked it up and carefully poured the dark green mixture into a shallow pan.

"*Brav!*" Milo said. "Now I will show you how the quality index is measured."

Drawing out a thin piece of wire, Milo strung it across the length of the room. Then, to Jack's astonishment, the professor took the list of names and carefully dipped each page into the pan. Jack expected the soaked paper to fall apart, but Milo drew each page out whole. Using metal clothespins, he clipped the papers onto the hanging wire to dry, then settled into the chair across from Jack. The room was silent except for the sound of droplets splattering on the metal drip pans.

Milo finally spoke, saying, "It will take time for them to dry. Since we have a moment, you will perhaps allow me to share a story about myself?"

"I'd like that," said Jack eagerly.

"Many years ago I went home to tell my mother I had fallen in love and was going to marry. I told her I would bring home three women, and she should guess which one I have chosen for my bride. So the next day, I sat the women down on the couch of my mother, and, *ja*, they began to talk and visit. When I asked which she thought I would marry, she chose the one in the middle. '*Fantastisch Mama!*' I said, 'How did you know?' and she replied, 'I don't like her.'"

A dry chuckle rumbled in Milo's chest, causing the scientist's shoulders to shake. He continued to tremble with laughter, finally removing his glasses to wipe his eyes with the white handkerchief he'd pulled from inside his lab coat.

Jack laughed as well, although more at Milo's reaction than at the joke itself.

"How are you going to tie that into the training?" Jack finally asked, trying to remember the last time he'd really laughed like that.

"Not *everything* is about the training, Jack," Milo said, shaking his head in amusement. "Only remember this: when building relationships, business will often be the last thing you discuss."

Milo went to check on the papers. "They are finished," he called out.

Jack heard the snapping of the clothespins, and Milo returned holding the sheaf of papers in his hands. Milo then looked over the results with grunts of surprise and interest. When he placed the stack in a metal pan on the table, Jack noticed that a different colored bar had appeared across each name.

"You have a population of 556 and a quality index of 2,349," Milo reported.

"Is that good?" Jack asked.

Milo pursed his lips and turned the palm of his hand in a so-so gesture. "It is an average quality index, but you do not nurture it so its potential is largely wasted."

Pulling out a small white packet from one of the containers, Milo tore it open and poured a cinnamon-colored powder into a beaker filled with a yellow liquid. He drained the contents of the beaker into a tube, and the mixture raced across the twisted glass and emptied into the metal pan where the stack of color-coded papers sat. As the liquid splashed onto the paper, an explosion of thick powdery smoke filled the room. Jack coughed and fanned away the smoke with his arms. As the smoke dissipated, he saw Milo beaming down at a large book.

"What is it?" Jack managed to croak out, moving forward to get a better look.

"Each city has its own telephone directory, no?" he said. "This is yours."

As Jack picked up the book, he realized the colors from the list now divided the telephone directory into five different sections. He opened the cover of the book and began leafing through the red-bordered pages at the front.

"Uh, I hate to burst your bubble, but I don't know these people," Jack said.

Milo directed him back to the cover page at the beginning of the section and Jack read the heading:

Level 0: Non resident

Do I have data?

"Level zero relationships are pieces of data. You have a name or other information, but you have no interaction," the professor explained.

"Like contacts in a database or names on a mailing list?" Jack asked.

"*Ja*, you have information that could assist you in contacting them, but you do not have a relationship with them," Milo explained.

Jack flipped through the pages to the "W's" and found Will Clay listed as a level zero.

He doesn't even factor into my quality index, Jack realized.

"So, to raise a relationship from a level zero to a level one, you must have interaction," Milo said, flipping over to the green section.

Jack read the cover sheet for the green section:

Level 1: Tourist

Have we had at least one positive interaction?

Jack recognized most of the names as he skimmed through the green pages, but then he stopped, looking up at Milo questioningly.

"Mary Webb?"

Milo's large eyes squinted behind his glasses. Then he snapped his fingers and said triumphantly, "You met Mary last week at a trade show in Las Vegas."

"You're right," Jack said, suddenly recalling the small, dark-haired woman bursting with energy. "I have a conference call set up with her tomorrow."

As Jack continued to read through the names, he saw a couple of new clients, several people he'd met at business functions and others he interacted with in the course of his day-to-day work. He had talked to them once or twice, but while he knew their names and the businesses they worked for, Jack suddenly realized that that was all he knew about them.

"So, tell me this, why do you think we call them tourists?" Milo asked.

Jack thought about this for a moment before replying. "They're just visiting my city, not necessarily moving in. To them I'm like the guy standing on the sidewalk trying to sell them a five-dollar watch, and they'll be suspicious of my motives until we get to know each other better."

"Wunderbar!" Milo exclaimed, clearly pleased with Jack's response.

Then flipping through the directory's pages, he turned to the title page of the next section:

Level 2: Renter

Have we had multiple positive interactions?

"Now we move to your level two relationships. We call them renters."

Skimming through the blue-bordered pages, Jack saw the majority of his renters were Dillon-Parker clients or vendors.

"Judging from the people in here, a level two can be a good level for business?" Jack asked hesitantly.

He knew each person listed and had done business with many of them, but he couldn't shake an uneasy feeling as he read through their names.

"That is right. Many transactions take place at this level, but they are usually based on price or performance alone."

Coming across Oscar Northcutt's name, Jack's stomach turned. Oscar was the general manager of Taylor & Taylor and a brand-new client. They'd missed a deadline for his first product launch earlier that week, and Jack was willing to bet that when the updated version of this directory came out, Oscar wouldn't even be listed.

Accurately interpreting Jack's expression, Milo added, "Always remember, level two relationships will remain strong only if expectations are met or exceeded. They have made a temporary investment in your city, but if your performance doesn't meet their expectations, they will leave as soon as their contract expires."

As Jack turned to the orange pages in the back, he noticed that each section was getting progressively smaller.

He read the title page for the level three section:

Level 3: Homeowner

```
Do we share an established Learn, Serve, Grow cycle?
```

On the first page he saw Gary Cabrera, a vendor who'd been supplying them with computer hardware since they'd first opened. A couple of pages in, he saw Holly Thayer and Don Gillespie, two of Dillon-Parker's largest clients. His accountant was listed as well as his close friends and a few neighbors.

"Consider this: What separates a homeowner from a renter?" Milo asked.

"Homeowners are obviously planning on being around for a while," Jack replied. Then, thinking it through a little more, he added, "They've invested in the relationship."

"That is right," Milo said approvingly. "You share an established Learn, Serve, Grow cycle with your homeowners. Because you genuinely like and trust this group, you consistently learn about their needs and serve their interests."

"But what's higher than this? Who's more invested in a city than a homeowner?" Jack asked, flipping to the very back of the book.

He read the cover of the silver-colored pages:

```
Level 4:  Developer
Do we give each other access to our time,
      influence, and resources?
```

Jack's list of developers wasn't long, but every indispensable person in his professional and personal life was listed.

At the top, Jack saw the name of his wife. Grace had been through a financial hurricane the past four years, yet continued to stand by Jack even now as things were spinning out of control. Deep down, he knew that without her support there would have been no Dillon-Parker in the first place.

His business partner, Monty James, was listed as well. Monty had been with Jack since Dillon-Parker was only a dream, and he had an amazing ability to stay calm and focused during a crisis. Jack couldn't even begin to count the number of times Monty had saved the company's collective bacon.

Murray, his banker, was there as were Adam Stringham and Heidi Lyon. Adam and Heidi both owned businesses that had strategically partnered with Dillon-Parker, and Jack estimated that almost thirty percent of his new business was coming from those two sources.

"Level four relationships are developers," Milo explained. "They are active in working toward the success of your city, and they trust you with high level access to their time, influence, and resources."

"High level access?" Jack asked.

"*Ja*, not unlimited access, but close. For example, level fours would rearrange their schedule to fit you in: *time*. They would introduce you to significant individuals inside their city: *influence*. During a cash flow emergency you could borrow a large sum of money from them: *resources*."

The description fit the group well. Looking through their names, Jack realized he would do almost anything for this group, and they'd do the same for him.

Milo closed the book, its heavy pages coming together with a soft thud. "Now I ask you this: What is the purpose of defining the relationship levels? How is it useful?"

Milo instantly had Jack's undivided attention. He'd been wondering that very thing.

"Let us look at an example. Tell me, what is your relationship level with Will Clay?"

"A level zero. I only have data."

"To increase your level of relationship, what is it you must you do?" Milo asked.

Thinking back to Milo's criteria for a level one, Jack said, "I need a positive interaction." Suddenly the pieces of the puzzle started sliding into place. "And the best place to do that is in a pool!"

"Then?" Milo prompted.

"Find more ways to interact with him," Jack finished slowly, "and begin the Learn, Serve, Grow cycle."

"*Korrekt!* Just as measuring the speed of your running allowed you to set goals to progress to a higher level, measuring your current relationship power with an individual becomes your guide to increasing it."

The droplets of rain began to pound more heavily against the roof, and a web of lightning lit up the night sky.

Milo moved over to the window and invited Jack to join him there. "You have felt unable to tap into the power of relationships just as the ancients were powerless to capture the power in lightning?"

Jack nodded and Milo held out a golden key. Engraved on its surface was *Measure Influence.*

"As you set specific goals to increase the quantity and quality of your relationships, you will have the ability to focus your scattered bits of influence into a laser."

Another bolt of lightning struck.

"You will have learned how to harness your lightning," Milo concluded.

15

Capitol Hill

The fat is not to be had without labor.

—Irish Proverb

A roll of thunder shook the house, and Jack suddenly found himself standing in front of an enormous granite building. Carved into the stone wall in front of him were the words "State Capitol." Inhaling the crisp autumn air, a smile spread across his face. Jack loved this time of year; it was when he felt most alive.

As he stood enjoying the fall colors, two large doors swung open, and a group of people exited the building. Some held microphones and were directing camera crews while others wore suits and carried portfolios. Instead of going down the stairs as Jack expected, the large contingent swung left and made a beeline straight for him. They began talking over each other as they gathered around him, shouting out questions.

One particularly aggressive woman forced her way to the front and thrust a microphone in Jack's face.

"Governor Green," she said, "according to data released today, your state ranks dead last in business growth, and there are a growing number of critics who think your policies are to blame. What's your response?"

Suddenly rooted to the concrete, Jack stared blankly at the jumble of microphones and an awkward silence ensued. A cameraman wearing a bright green T-shirt finally poked his face out from behind his camera and gave Jack a thumbs-up sign.

Recognizing Patrick, Jack regained the use of his voice. He held up a finger and said, "Let me get back to you on that."

Herding Patrick off a short distance, he growled through gritted teeth, "You turned me into a *governor?* Are you insane?"

"Now then, Governor Green, you're wasting precious time," Patrick said, easing his camera from his shoulder and placing it on the ground. "You've a state to be running."

"No, Patrick," Jack corrected him. "I've got a business to run."

"Well, as the CEO, you're also Dillon-Parker's governor, so you best be accepting that fact."

Looking over his shoulder at the reporters and lobbyists, Jack began to panic at the prospect of appearing on the ten o'clock news sounding like a complete idiot.

"What should I say?" he asked.

Patrick stroked his chin as he considered the question. "Just tell them you've hired a new advisor known for turning things about. But hurry, lad; we've much to do yet."

Returning to the reporters, Jack gave the statement then escaped the volley of questions that immediately erupted. He followed Patrick across the marble floor of the portico into the building, and they managed to catch an open elevator. Patrick pushed the button for the top floor, and the elevator doors opened a few moments later to reveal a well-furnished lobby. Patrick led Jack to a spacious office set in the back.

Jack was immediately drawn to an ornate desk in the center of the room that had several documents strewn across it. As he examined them, Jack saw each one had an embossed state seal and *Governor Jackson Green* scrawled across the signature line.

"A governor huh?" Jack said, sitting back in the desk's tall leather chair and clasping his hands behind his head. "I could get used to this."

"Well, before you be getting too big for your britches, Governor, I'll need to be showing you something."

Pulling back a heavy curtain that ran along one side of the office, Patrick released a flood of sunlight into the dim room. The window he'd uncovered filled an entire wall, and through it Jack saw a sprawling valley filled with different cities. He went over to the window to get a better look at the closest city, and although he couldn't make out the details, his first impression was not positive.

Patrick retrieved a pair of binoculars from the desk drawer and handed them to Jack. Looking through them, he had a clear view of a green signpost that read Advertising Avenue and Designer Row. Jack dropped the binoculars and stared at them in amazement.

"Now, don't be telling me after all you've been through this night that a powerful pair of binoculars is going to be surprising you," Patrick commented, amused.

Good point, Jack thought.

He adjusted the binoculars, and began sweeping through the streets of the city. With a sinking feeling, he realized that not only was it small, but most of it was in serious disrepair. Its few large buildings were either old or hopelessly generic, and its streets were so narrow that even small amounts of traffic made them feel congested. As Jack scanned through the suburbs, business districts, and downtown areas, he did see a couple of decent shops and one or two nice neighborhoods, but they did little to offset the negatives.

"This isn't my city, is it?" Jack asked, not sure he wanted to know.

Patrick shrugged his shoulders sadly. "Aye, that it is. All the time you've been spending in the coliseum has taken its toll."

Jack looked over the city again, suddenly flooded with an overpowering urge to roll up his sleeves and get to work immediately.

"But as the governor, you've more than just your own city to be worrying about," Patrick reminded him. Pointing to a nearby valley, he said "Yonder is Monty's city. And see there? Tucked away at the foot of those mountains? Those are the cities of your three best salespeople. Every Dillion-Parker city is here somewhere, and as the governor 'tis your duty to establish statewide systems and standards that ensure the growth and prosperity of them all. Until you do this, you'll be doing little more than managing chaos."

"Systems and standards?" Jack asked, confused.

"Aye. Take another look." Jack looked through the binoculars again and Patrick asked. "Do you see a freeway, highway or even a dirt road connecting one city to the others?"

Concerned, Jack admitted he didn't see anything like that.

"One of the tools Dillion-Parker is short on is a way to help its mayors share their knowledge and influence. By not having a shared system for information and collaboration, your mayors don't have the access they need to adequately manage their cities."

Taking a deep breath, Patrick plunged in again. He explained that another responsibility of a governor was to establish the standards by which each city was to be judged. As things stood, even if a mayor was doing a brilliant job managing their city, Jack had no way of knowing it. Patrick told him that without an agreed upon expectation, there could be no real accountability. Until the cities inside Jack's state had a uniform code and were held to a common standard, he'd never be a true governor.

"A good politician, perhaps, but never a governor," Patrick concluded.

Patrick then pointed to a distant disc of shining water. Through the binoculars, Jack saw a beautiful city nestled on the edge of the massive lake.

"Whose city is that?" Jack asked in awe.

"Kimberly Burke's. When it comes to governing a city that woman's a wonder," Patrick said admiringly. "How long has she been with you?"

"Just a couple of weeks. I didn't have much to do with her hiring," Jack responded, adjusting the binoculars and zooming in on the shady parks, inviting neighborhoods, and stunning business district of the far-off city.

"If you'd had a system that measured her population and quality index, you'd have thanked the stars above the day she was hired. She's a population of 934 and a quality index of 4,056," Patrick said, clearly impressed.

"Four thousand," Jack gasped. "That's almost double mine!"

"Nothing personal, lad, but when you get home I wouldn't be setting your score up as the benchmark," Patrick said with a wry grin. "Kimberly's a brilliant mayor, make no mistake about that. The lass not only continually adds to her population, but works to increase the quality of each relationship. Yet, as things stand, Kimberly's city can only play a limited role in Dillon-Parker's success because the company has no systems or standards. When it comes to building her city, she's on her own."

Patrick went over to the desk, pulled out a small box from one of the drawers and opened it. Inside was a gold key that bore the inscription *Establish City Systems and Standards* and a small card that Patrick picked up and handed to Jack.

The card had the following action items listed :

```
Governor's Checklist

1. Create systems that measure the popula-
   tion and quality index of each city.

2. Build roads and freeways that connect
   the cities and allow them to share their
   influence and resources.

3. Develop general standards for everything
   from how often residents are contacted
   to how quickly a city should grow to
   avoid congestion.
```

Pointing to his city, Jack protested, "How am I supposed to teach my staff how to be mayors? Just look at my city. My welcome sign probably says 'Welcome to Parasite Valley. Population: Two less than yesterday.'"

Patrick took a seat in a small alcove near the window and invited Jack to join him. "I know that all this can feel a wee bit overwhelming, but take heart. If I can be making the change, anyone can."

Patrick then picked up the thread of his story where he'd left off earlier in the evening. "I arrived on the shores of this country starving and penniless, and the moment my feet touched American soil, I began my search for work. In the beginning, I could only get factory work, making wages that barely kept us alive," Patrick frowned at the memory. "'Twas was a bitter thing for me to have rescued my family from famine only to see them live in squalor. It put me into quite a temper, I can tell you that. But I was determined to get ahead, and soon enough I was a full-fledged gladiator, fighting tooth and nail in the coliseum."

As he spoke, Patrick's face took on a hard expression that Jack had never seen before. At that moment, he could picture him waging his battle against his opponents, no matter who he hurt in the process.

"Lad, your city looks like a thriving metropolis compared to the depths mine had sunk to. People were immigrating out of it like 'twas hell itself!" Patrick said, shaking his head at the memory.

"Through grit and hard work, I eventually scrimped enough to begin a small manufacturing establishment of my own," he continued, "A prize-winning fighter in the price and performance wars. But then I met your great-great grandfather and things began to change. You see, I was a supplier for his small shop, and I remember being very critical of the way he ran his business. I told Molly he was a sentimental fool, but like everyone else who knew George, he eventually won me over. Sure, he was one of the rare ones—a lad as genuinely interested in the success of others as he was in his own. As time went on, instead of going out of business as I expected, his shop began to prosper. After watching this for a time, I finally worked up the courage to ask him about it."

Jack could picture the two men, sitting together by the fire with George sifting through his keys as he explained the principles of influence to Patrick.

"From that day on, we began building our cities together and it didn't take us long to realize that there wasn't a thing in the world we couldn't accomplish with the help of other people. George sold his shop to join me as my partner, and within ten years our team of broken-down Irish immigrants had become one of the finest workforces in all of America—proving you didn't have to beat down your employees, competitors, and clients to make profit."

Jack had studied enough about their company to know the rest of the story. They had been successful beyond belief.

"Now, lad, I've an important question to ask you."

"You're not going to dump me back into the coliseum if I get it wrong, are you?" Jack asked, only half-joking.

"Don't worry, lad. You're sure to be knowing the answer," Patrick reassured him. "What would you say is the difference between a governor and a gladiator?"

Jack took plenty of time to gather his thoughts, replaying the lessons of the evening in his mind.

"Gladiators make self-preservation their primary concern and personal victory their highest ambition. On the other hand, governors make the success of their mayors, as well as the residents inside their own city of influence, their highest priority."

"So what are your responsibilities as a governor—the leader of your company?" Patrick asked.

Jack scanned the distant cities on the horizon.

"Governors help each city mayor become accountable to systems and standards designed to keep their populations growing and safe," he finally responded.

"Aye, you've got it." Patrick pointed to Jack's city and said, "I can promise you one thing. There's nothing quite like sitting in front of these windows and watching the magic of relationships transform your little valley."

As Jack imagined this, he felt a new level of commitment well up inside him.

"And that's the secret, lad. Security isn't complicated and it isn't about money. Real security is reserved for the rare few who care enough to build cities that give back to the people that live inside of them."

It was as if all the lessons had found their position and locked perfectly into place.

"So, we've reached the end?" Jack asked.

"Aye, just about, Governor Green. All that remains is your final exam."

16

Will Clay

You'll never plow a field by turning it over in your mind.

—Irish Proverb

“The time has come for you to be applying what you've learned,” Patrick told him. “Are you ready?”

Jack nodded. *Well, as ready as I'll ever be,* he thought.

“Tell me this, then. How would you go about building a relationship with Will Clay?”

Jack sighed with relief; this question he could answer. “Right now all I have is data. To reach a level one, I need to find a pool where I can get to know him,” he replied.

“Right you are! Let's see if we can uncover a few of Will's pools,” Patrick suggested.

They turned away from the window and went back to the ornate desk in the center of the room. Jack took a seat in front of the computer, and the Clay and Chagall website soon filled the screen. As Jack scanned through the information, he reported that Clay and Chagall was a national firm, divided into partners, associates, and hourly workers. The partners divided the firm's responsibilities between them, and Will was the partner responsible for marketing and design.

“What else?” Patrick asked.

Jack clicked into the company biographies, and a full-length picture of Will Clay appeared. He was dressed in an expensive suit, and his intense expression left no doubt as to his legal prowess.

"His bio says he's on the board of the local homeless shelter, and that he enjoys traveling and fishing. Hey, we graduated from the same university," Jack replied. He looked at the screen thoughtfully. "You know, it's been a while since I've attended the booster club meetings. I wonder if Will is a member?"

Patrick shrugged. "'Tis a good idea, but a bit slow for tonight's needs. A better place to begin may be your current city residents. Let's see if any of them already have a relationship with Will."

A text box suddenly appeared on the computer screen, its cursor blinking in front of the words "Influence Search." Jack noted with amazement that the Foundation apparently had its own search engine.

"Go ahead, lad. Type in Will Clay's name and see if there's a match," Patrick prompted.

Jack typed in the name, and when the screen refreshed it displayed three results. The first line listed David Edwards (level 1), the second line listed James Olson (level 2), and the third line listed Maggie Wilkinson (level 3).

"Maggie has a level three relationship with Will Clay? Are you serious?"

"The world's a much smaller place than you'd be imagining," Patrick told him. "His biography said he was a diehard fisherman."

"He's at her pool, isn't he?" Jack was pacing the room now, unable to control his excitement. He felt like he'd just received a carbonation transfusion directly into his veins.

"He wouldn't dream of missing it," Patrick replied, allowing himself a satisfied smile.

"And that's why you chose her to be one of my trainers?" Jack asked.

"You'll be finding out soon enough that a high-level relationship doesn't just bless you once, but over and over again."

Without warning, Jack found himself standing inside the Fish Village Store, fully outfitted in a vest and waders with a fishing pole in one hand and a net in the other.

I guess I'm going fishing, he thought.

Jack discovered Patrick one aisle over, examining a massive display of flies as well as an assortment of colorful feathers and fur to tie them with.

"If you guys are expecting me to tie my own fly, you can just forget it," Jack said firmly.

"Don't worry, lad," Patrick said. "Maggie'll set you up right and tight."

They heard Maggie's voice and soon she was hurrying down the aisle toward them.

"You're back!" she said.

"Aye, and we're in need of a favor, lass," Patrick answered. "How much longer is your Fattest Fish Competition running?"

Maggie checked her watch and responded, "There's less than an hour left."

"Well then, could you be pointing us in the direction of the best fishing spot around here?"

"What kind of fish are you wanting to catch, Patrick?" Maggie asked, a sparkle coming into her eyes.

"One answering to the name of Will Clay. I've heard he has some heavy branding and design needs," Patrick replied with a wink.

Maggie led them through a side door to the deck. Stopping at the top of a stairway, she pointed to the trailhead marker that stood a few feet from the bottom step.

"That particular fish is quite a creature of habit," Maggie said. "His favorite spot is just down that trail a ways. Keep going until you see a big blue spruce."

"Now, wait just a second," Jack broke in, backing away from the stairway. "I fished once or twice in Boy Scouts, but that was more than twenty years ago!"

Jack felt relatively comfortable with some of the equipment, but some of it was completely foreign.

Maggie launched into a two-minute speed orientation. She showed Jack how to attach the line and leader to the front of his rod and explained how to use the floatant and weights. She finished by dropping a pair of nippers into his vest pocket and telling him to use them to retrieve the fly once he caught a fish.

"You're all set," Maggie said. "Good luck!"

Unable to think of a way to stall for more time, Jack trudged down the stairs like he'd just received a death sentence. They followed the tree-lined path and located the spruce. Just as Maggie had predicted, Will Clay was there, knee-deep in the water and casting out over the river.

Jack stopped again, worry erupting in his stomach like a volcano. As much as he wanted to meet Will Clay, he was equally terrified of messing up.

"You're not just going to throw me into this, are you?" he whispered to Patrick.

"Action cuts down the suffering by a half, lad" Patrick replied, gently pushing him forward. "You've a firm grasp on the principles—now it's just a matter of doing what you know."

Taking a deep breath, Jack walked to the bank and waded out into the river. He found a spot directly across from where Will Clay stood, and Will gave him a friendly nod. Taking a firm grip on his pole, Jack tried to cast his line, but the momentum of his swing caused him to lose his balance and he fell face first into the water. He emerged sputtering, and then to his horror, realized his waders were filling with water and the pull of the current was dragging him downriver.

When Will realized Jack was in trouble, he instantly sprang to his aid. He rescued Jack's pole and pulled him out of the river onto the bank. Water dripping from their faces and clothes, the two men worked to get Jack's boots and waders off and empty them.

When they'd finished, Will looked at Jack with some amusement, "It's been awhile?" he asked.

"How'd you guess?" Jack said, his face hot with embarrassment. "I think I was twelve the last time I did this."

"Then it's just a matter of remembering, isn't it?" Will replied.

After helping him get back into his waders, he persuaded Jack to give it another try. Under Will's watchful eye, Jack practiced throwing his line.

"You're casting it like a pitcher," Will said, laughing. He took Jack's arm and guided it in a slow arc. "Go easy."

"Throwing a baseball comes more naturally, I guess," Jack replied.

They stood in silence for a while, the river ebbing and flowing between them, their lines whipping back and forth through the air.

Finally, Jack gathered up his courage and asked, "You're Will Clay, aren't you? With Clay and Chagall?"

Will looked up from reeling in his line. "Why, yes I am," he said, surprised.

Jack attempted to cast out again. This time he was too easy and the line dropped barely a foot in front of him.

"Then I'd better hold off telling you my latest lawyer joke," he said, reeling in his line again.

Will rolled his eyes. "You won't come up with anything I haven't already heard from my 'friends' down at the Oak Grove Shelter. You would think they'd have some compassion, but those do-gooders are ruthless. I'm on their board of directors, and lately it's been more stressful than an IRS audit."

"Why?" Jack asked.

"You don't even want to know," Will assured him.

The image of Kris listening intently to his problems flashed through Jack's mind. "Sure I do. Tell me about it."

Will looked at Jack skeptically, but must have sensed his interest was sincere because he launched into a vivid description of how the board had bamboozled him into taking responsibility for getting the auction items for their annual fundraiser. They wanted him to find at least fifty items, each of a $200 value or more.

"Working with a law firm, I don't have many connections in the retail world," Will said. "I feel like my assistant and I have been working on it nonstop."

"Any luck?" Jack asked.

"It's a dog-eat-dog world out there," Will answered with a grimace. "It's been a lot harder than I thought."

Jack recognized the strained expression on Will's face. It was the same one he saw in the mirror every morning, and he began thinking about ways he could help.

As if someone had pressed a cosmic pause button, everything around Jack suddenly froze. Patrick materialized beside him wearing a hat covered with baits and lures.

"How are you faring?"

"I never would've thought Will Clay was so personable," Jack replied. "He not only helped me when I fell, but he took the time to give me some pointers." Looking over to where Will stood in the river, his line frozen in midair, Jack concluded, "He's the kind of person you actually want to help."

"Fine, lad. Now how can you lend a hand?" Patrick asked.

Jack absently clasped and unclasped the pole with his fingers. "He needs items for a fundraiser. I could have the company donate some of it, but . . ."

"At the rate you're losing money, you best not try and foot the entire bill yourself," Patrick finished for him. "But you do be having other resources. What about the people inside your city of influence?"

"I'm way ahead of you. I was just about to say that I have strong relationships with a couple of specialty laptop and small-electronics providers."

"My work has not been in vain!" Patrick exclaimed, holding up his hands in triumph.

"I haven't been totally out to lunch this whole time," responded Jack, half pleased, half irritated with Patrick's reaction.

Apparently satisfied, Patrick snapped his fingers and disappeared. Time unfroze and Will repeated himself again, as if feeding Jack his cue.

"It's a dog-eat-dog world out there. It's been a lot harder than I thought."

Will's shoulders slumped as he looked out over the water.

"You know," Jack said casually, reeling in his line, "I have some wholesale connections with my work. I could make a couple of calls. I'm sure they'd be glad to get the write-off on their taxes."

"Really?" Will said, his eyes widening in surprise. "I mean, that would be great, but I couldn't ask you to do that."

"You didn't ask, I'm offering. Consider it a fair trade for saving me from a watery grave," Jack replied, dismissing it with a shrug.

A good feeling was beginning to spread over Jack, and he realized he didn't even care if Will Clay reciprocated his generosity.

Will waded over to where Jack stood and shook his hand enthusiastically. "I can't tell you how much I appreciate this."

"It's not a big deal. I talk to those guys every day. I only wish I could do more." Then Jack had a sudden stroke of inspiration. "In fact, maybe I can. My Uncle Mac is one of the fastest-talking cattle auctioneers you've ever seen. Do you need an auctioneer?"

"Yes!" Will practically shouted. "It's been one of our biggest snags. We could pay him."

"I'll let you work that out with him. He's probably home right now. Let me give him a call."

He borrowed Will's cell phone and made the call. After briefly explaining the situation to his uncle, he handed the phone back to Will. Within minutes, Will and Mac had worked out the details.

"I'll give my electronics guys a call tomorrow and let you know what they say," Jack told Will when he'd finished.

Will pulled a business card from a vest pocket and handed it to Jack. "Just tell my assistant who you are and what you're calling about, and she'll put you right through." Will suddenly stopped and began to chuckle. "By the way, what's your name?"

"Jack."

"Thanks again, Jack."

They continued to fish, Will calling out pointers as Jack worked on his casting.

"I just thought of something," Will said. "We have two extra seats at our table at the fundraiser. Do you and your wife want to join us?"

Jack paused to consider this. "I think I'd like to see those ruthless do-gooders in action," he said with a grin. "We'll be there."

Suddenly there was a splash in the river.

"I think you got one!" Will cried out in astonishment.

He called out frantic instructions as Jack doggedly hung on to the pole. Finally, Jack thrust the pole into Will's hands, and watched him reel in an enormous silver trout. By the time it was flopping around in the net, both men were soaked and laughing.

Insisting he didn't want to clean it, Jack finally persuaded Will to take the fish. His pole in one hand and the fish in the other, Will thanked Jack again and headed back toward Fish Village. As soon as Will was out of sight, Patrick reappeared on a nearby rock.

"Well, that was . . . different," Jack said.

"Didn't it feel right to you, lad?" Patrick asked.

Jack took a seat on a nearby rock. "To help someone just because they need the help? Yeah, it felt right."

"Do you see how twisting the conversation into a sales pitch for your business would've changed the whole feeling?" Patrick asked. "And yet you did help your business."

Surprised, Jack looked up from where he sat pulling off his waders. "I did? But he doesn't even know what I do. I didn't even mention it."

Patrick gave Jack a knowing look.

"Come now, lad, eventually he'll be asking you what you do for a living, and when he does, who'll he think of first when his firm needs a bit of branding assistance?" Patrick said. "And even if you never see a penny, a governor's growth doesn't always be coming in the form of financial gain. Even if Will never does business with Dillon-Parker, you still made a new friend and learned something about fishing."

As they stacked the poles and tackle underneath one of the pine trees, Patrick also pointed out that Will had invited Jack to a pool, which not only gave him an opportunity to get to know Will better but also offered him the chance to connect with a whole new group of people.

"You see, when you focus on building relationships 'just because,' people naturally reciprocate — and the business side of things tends to take care of itself."

17.

Two Roads

The longest road out is the shortest road home.

—Irish Proverb

T he alarm on Patrick's phone began to beep, and he motioned for Jack to follow him. "Time marches on! We'd best be off," he said.

As they walked forward there was a bright flash, and Jack suddenly found himself standing on a dirt road. Ten feet ahead of him the path forked in two different directions.

"Why do I feel like I just landed in a Robert Frost poem?" Jack asked, his gaze shifting between the two paths.

The path to the right wound its way along a tree-lined slope and disappeared into a valley of rolling green hills, while the narrow brick-paved path to the left snaked up a steep incline.

"Which one do I take?" he asked.

"I knew a young lass named Alice who once asked that same question of a cat," Patrick said conversationally, climbing on one of the railings of the wooden fence that lined the road.

Jack rolled his eyes. "It didn't happen to be a Cheshire cat, did it?"

"Aye, it was!" Patrick exclaimed, startled. "Have you met Miss Alice?"

Jack just shook his head.

"No? Well, the way she tells it, when she asked the cat which path she should be taking, he said that depended entirely on where she was wanting to end up. Miss Alice told him she didn't much care so long as she arrived somewhere."

"And what did the cat say?" Jack asked, climbing up beside Patrick, intrigued in spite of himself.

Patrick inspected his fingernails closely. "He told Miss Alice if she didn't care where she ended up, it didn't much matter which way she went."

Jack gave Patrick a long look. "Are you asking me where I want to end up? What are my choices?"

"The road yonder is your first choice," Patrick said pointing down the shady pathway winding through a lush valley.

Jack felt a strange sense of nostalgia as he looked down the lane. It was as though he had arrived at this intersection a thousand times before, and this was the path he'd always taken.

"It looks so familiar," he told Patrick.

"That's because you've been down that path already," Patrick replied, confirming Jack's suspicions. "That's the road to the coliseum."

Jack ventured over to the trailhead of the second path. "And this one?" he asked, his gaze lingering on the spot where the brick pathway disappeared into the steep mountainside.

Patrick jumped off the fence and went to stand beside Jack. "If you've a mind to climb it, that would be the path to Relationship Summit. At its peak, you'll find safe passage into every city of influence, but I'll be warning you now, 'tis the longer, more demanding path."

It was obvious to Jack why he had always chosen the first road. One promised a pleasant, easy walk, while the other guaranteed an intense climb.

Patrick looked as serious as Jack had ever seen him. "Make no mistake about it, these roads are real. You can follow the path to the coliseum, hoping to become a champion gladiator fighting to the death over price and performance, or you can decide now to become a governor and begin gathering together the relationships that'll sustain you through a lifetime."

Jack bit his lip as he looked back and forth between the two roads, but deep down he knew he'd already made his decision. He took the left fork and began climbing up the mountainous path.

"I'll be waiting for you at the summit," Patrick called out, waving him on.

The climb was steep from the start, stretching ever upward, and the loose rocks, which eventually replaced the brick path, shifted under his feet and slowed his progress. Although Jack knew he'd made the right decision, he began to wonder if he had the stamina to reach the top. His work schedule hadn't allowed for much in the way of exercise lately, and he was paying a serious price for it now.

As the sun beat down hotter and hotter, his breathing became labored, and a fierce burning sensation spread throughout his chest. At the crest of the first hill, he saw an enormous peak looming up in front of him, the path running a jagged progression up the mountain. As Jack stared up at it, he saw the silhouettes of other people farther along the path and realized others were making the same journey.

The path alternated between sharp, rocky ledges, where the trees bent almost in half as they struggled to remain parallel to the mountainside, and occasional flat stretches through sunken mountain meadows. Jack took several detours off the beaten path to rest his feet on the thick mountain grass.

Near the peak, he had to navigate fields of boulders and stretches of glacier snow before approaching the final climb to the summit. Jack wasn't sure how many hours had passed, but he was pretty sure his legs couldn't hold out much longer. Using his last ounce of energy, he crested the final ridge and a spectacular vista burst out before him.

Jack caught his breath in wonder as he lowered his exhausted body to the flat stone ledge, his gaze never leaving the valley below. As he visually traced the route of the first path, he said to himself, "It's just a big circle. The path doesn't go anywhere but back to the coliseum."

He didn't hear Patrick come up behind him, but wasn't surprised to hear his voice.

"Where else would daily battles fighting over price and performance lead?" Patrick asked as he took a seat next to Jack.

"To more daily battles," Jack answered, feeling like he was finally beginning to really understand. He leaned back on his elbows and absently stared at the large formations of clouds congregating along the skyline. "I have to admit, in the beginning, battling in the coliseum was kind of a rush. You really do believe if you just get in there and fight hard enough, you'll eventually find a way to win every battle."

A blast of trumpets rang out from a huge stone structure below and the throbbing drumbeats let the audience know that the games were about to begin. Patrick removed the binoculars that hung around his neck and handed them to Jack. Focusing them on the playing field, Jack watched as a gladiator slowly limped to the center of the field and raised his sword with great effort. The crowd responded with a deafening roar.

Jack felt deep empathy mixed with frustration as he watched the battle begin. Slaves appeared on opposite sides of the arena, pulling on the leashes of two snarling wolves. As they released the wolves, the crowd let out a scream of approval. The animals began to circle the gladiator until one finally attacked.

"Why is he fighting wolves?" Jack asked. "Where are the other gladiators?"

"'Tis not only competitors that kill businesses," Patrick replied. "That particular lad happens to be battling financial reversals from product defects, but there are a thousand different kinds of wolves."

Jack watched the gladiator strike one wolf down, but behind him, the other one lunged, ripping into the gladiator's side with its sharp teeth. The gladiator quickly rolled out of its reach and sprang back to his feet. As the animal charged forward, the gladiator picked up a javelin from the ground and hurled it into the face of the beast. The wolf went down in a cloud of dust, sending the crowd into a frenzy and they chanted the gladiator's name.

"Another gladiator hailed as a hero," Patrick observed, his face tense.

"Until tomorrow," Jack responded grimly.

As Jack scanned the surrounding area, something else caught his attention. He noticed the fields that crisscrossed the landscape were filled with gray slabs. When Jack asked what they were, Patrick explained they were graveyards.

Jack looked sick. "You don't mean . . ."

The crowd let out another roar, and Jack lifted the binoculars to see two slaves carrying the gladiator's body off the field.

"Look over there," Patrick said.

Jack focused the binoculars on the spot where Patrick was pointing just in time to see a new tombstone appear in the corner of the graveyard.

"That gladiator put everything he had into the battle, but it wasn't enough," Patrick explained, turning away from the scene below.

"But there must be tens of thousands of tombstones down there," Jack protested.

"Aye, lad, you know that more than half of all businesses fail in the first four years; it's just that you usually don't get a front-row seat to the funerals."

Patrick sat silently, his face working to contain the emotions he was feeling. "I'm sick of the sight, though it be familiar enough," he said. "These eager lads and lasses walk into the arena and surround themselves with relationships based solely on price or performance. Whether their business lives or dies makes no difference to the crowd; they scream just as loud when the wolves win."

A cheer went up from the coliseum as another gladiator was struck down.

"The coliseum has some great gladiators who will fight tooth and nail," Patrick finished, "but most will end up beneath a tombstone, killed by a wolf or by a younger, smarter opponent," Patrick said.

"Who says the path to Relationship Summit is harder?" Jack wondered.

"Aye, but 'tis a journey you'll have to be making over and over again," Patrick warned him. He walked over to the ledge, and looked down on the path Jack had just climbed. "Every step of your journey to Relationship Summit represented one of the actions of a governor. It may've been building a relationship 'just because,' measuring your levels of relationship, or building an effective pool."

Jack stood beside Patrick and looked down the path he'd just climbed. Although it was precarious, and climbing it had required all his strength, at least it wasn't infested with wild animals and gladiators trying to tear him apart.

"It wasn't easy," Jack said slowly. "I thought about turning back a couple of times, but now, looking at it from this perspective, I am glad that I was at least investing my effort in something meaningful instead of wasting my resources running in circles."

Patrick gave a quick nod of approval. "By choosing to build a city of influence, you'll increase in all the areas that a person *can* be wealthy— in your business, your family, your community, and your friendships."

Jack's gaze swept across the coliseum one last time.

"I've seen enough," he said, turning away from the cliff's edge.

18.

The City of Influence

'Tis afterwards that everything is understood.

—Irish Proverb

Patrick and Jack crossed to the other side of the summit, and hundreds of beautiful cities came into view. The sun was just beginning to set, and a soft glow bathed the cities in golden light. It was the most remarkable sight Jack had ever seen.

"Sure, this brings back a flood of memories," Patrick said with a faraway look in his eyes. "During my days as a governor, I watched over even more cities than this if you can believe it."

A high-pitched clanging sound suddenly rang out, and Jack turned to see a trolley emerge from a cavernous tunnel and glide toward them. Its apple-red paint and scalloped gold trim looked so out of place against the rugged mountainside that Jack wondered if the high altitude was causing his mind to play tricks on him. But the track that lay near his feet was unquestionably solid.

"Don't you think trolleys have a chipper sound, lad?" Patrick asked as the trolley pulled to a stop in front of them. "Like they're talking to you, saying, 'Top of the morning, and would you enjoy a ride?'"

"Where to next?" Jack asked as they grabbed the trolley's thick brass poles and stepped aboard.

"That's up to you, lad. By reaching the summit, you've now the privilege of visiting the city of your choice. I'd be honored to have you visit my own little township, if you'd like," Patrick suggested. "'Tisn't far, just down the mountain and across a valley or two."

Jack nodded. "I'd like that."

The bell clanged once more and they were off, the wind whistling through their ears as they sailed down the steep mountain slope; soon they were approaching Patrick's city. As they entered its borders, a feeling of peace and security engulfed Jack. Unlike the big cities where he'd lived most of his life, this one was consistently beautiful all the way through. In the lush landscape of the residential district, each home seemed alive with its own unique personality and style. The business and downtown districts were also exceptionally well kept and seemed to combine the energy of Time's Square with the warmth and charm of a European village.

As they entered the neighborhoods on the other side of the city, the trolley gradually slowed to a stop. Jack stepped off and found himself standing on a street lined with brick cottages and magnificent maple trees. As he and Patrick walked down the lane, Jack noticed that each home had a gold plate on the mailbox announcing its owner.

"Each of your trainers keeps a home inside my city," Patrick told him.

And sure enough, he saw Cordelia's house, then a few doors down he saw Kris's house and across the street was Angela's. In the end, the only house Jack didn't see was Ron's. When he asked about this, Patrick explained that Ron preferred to live downtown where there was a little more nightlife.

They stopped in front of a newly framed house where the smell of freshly cut wood still lingered in the air. Engraved on the mailbox in shiny black letters was the name *Jack Green*. Jack stopped in front of the building site and stood there for a long time.

"Did I pick the right spot, lad?" Patrick asked quietly.

"It's perfect. Thank you."

A small group of men and women came walking up the lane toward them. They were carrying flashlights and a small cooler, and when they saw Patrick, they called out to him.

"If you'll be excusing me, Jack, this won't take but a minute."

Patrick walked over to the group and appeared to be giving them directions. He pointed to the west then turned and pointed in the opposite direction. Jack assumed that Patrick said something funny next, because the whole group exploded with laughter.

When Patrick returned, Jack waited for a few moments, then finally blurted out, "What was all that about?"

"What's that, lad?" Patrick asked.

"I mean, what was the deal with all those people? Why did they have flashlights and food? Where are they going?" Suddenly Jack realized this was none of his business and stopped. "Sorry. I don't mean to be nosy."

Patrick gave Jack a warm smile and replied, "With the Irish, there's no such thing as nosy, just curious. But the answer to your question is to be found in the O'Flannery clan motto: 'Let Enemies Beware.'"

Jack laughed. "Oh, that's friendly! Who came up with that one, the Irish Grim Reaper?"

"Oh, but 'tis a strong motto indeed. Everyone has enemies that could harm their businesses, especially governors. The lads and lasses you saw me talking to are part of my neighborhood watch."

"Neighborhood watch?" Jack asked.

Patrick explained that governors and mayors still had to deal with gladiators and wolves just like everyone else. They struggled with dishonest competitors, bad investments, poor strategic decisions, and other disappointing setbacks. The difference was that those who'd built strong cities of influence never faced those challenges alone.

"The reason you rarely hear of gladiators or wolves doing serious damage to a mature city of influence is because they must not only contend with the mayor, but also with all the loyal residents who live there," Patrick explained.

Jack looked at the retreating forms of the neighborhood watch and realized that he wouldn't want to take that group on.

"Well, we'd best be getting to it, or we're going to be late," Patrick said.

"Late for what?" Jack asked.

Patrick smiled but refused to answer as they walked toward the end of the lane. A large brick mansion stood there, its warm yellow light spilling from diamond-paned windows onto the thick grass of the lawn. The gold plate on its mailbox bore the name *Patrick O'Flannery.*

Patrick opened the front door, and as Jack followed him into a darkened entryway, the lights flipped on and a group of voices yelled out, "Surprise!"

Jack had never been to a surprise party before, least of all one thrown for him. Surrounded by his new friends, he couldn't believe this many people—most of whom he'd never met before tonight—would care enough to put something like this together.

In the kitchen, Molly had prepared a feast for a king, complete with mouthwatering meat dishes, mounds of fruit and elaborate desserts. Everyone pitched in to help carry the platters of food to the long mahogany table. When they'd all taken their seats, Patrick stood at the head of the table and held up a glass.

"I want to welcome you all to Jack's graduation party. As you all know, we will be having a traditional Irish toast for just such important occasions," Patrick announced.

Everyone at the table lifted their glasses, and Jack followed suit.

"May the roof above us never fall in, and may the friends below it never fall out," Patrick said.

"Hear, hear!" everyone chorused.

The group sat down and instantly began chattering and bantering with each other. As the dinner progressed, all of them took a turn telling the others about their part in Jack's journey. Jack laughed right along with the rest of them, enjoying the retellings of his own experiences as much as they did. Then after they'd finished eating and had cleared the dishes, the trainers returned to the table, exchanging devious looks.

"Okay, what's going on?" asked Jack, looking around suspiciously. "I can tell when you guys are up to something."

Kris let out a hearty chuckle and said, "To keep up our skills, Patrick has introduced a little competition of sorts. We've all had the chance to learn a little about you tonight, and now we get the opportunity to see if we can serve you in some way."

Chase spoke up. "I'll go first," he said. "While I was doing my surveillance, I discovered that you have a serious cash flow problem, and, as a last resort, you've maxed out all of your credit cards. I think I've got just the man to help. He's an outside investor who likes to take on crazy, high-risk people like you. He'll be giving you a call."

Jack's mouth dropped open in amazement, but before he could say anything, Maggie began telling the group how she'd learned that Jack needed some advice on bankruptcy laws because a major client had recently gone under with a large invoice unpaid.

"I discussed the situation with Will Clay after the competition, and he jumped at the chance to give you a little free advice," Maggie finished. "Bankruptcy happens to be his specialty."

Jack felt his shoulders begin to relax for the first time in months.

Ron went next. "Jack, you were telling me that your daughter—the one who loves the story of the three pigs—has been struggling with her speech and is getting teased at school. Angela and I discussed it, and she called a couple of highly respected speech pathologists."

"I spoke with a number of them to find out the best thing to do," Angela added. "I e-mailed you their recommendations."

Mark went next, pulling out a slip of paper with two names and phone numbers scrawled on it. "I know a couple of CEOs who are looking into re-branding. Here are their names and numbers," he said, passing the paper to Jack. "I told them someone from your company would be calling them to set up a presentation."

The trainers continued to share their gifts until each had taken a turn.

"I don't know what to say," Jack offered.

He looked around the table in amazement. He had long since decided this wasn't a dream, but he could never have guessed things would turn out this well.

Patrick leaned over and elbowed Jack. "The end of a feast is better than the beginning of a fight, eh? Tell me now, Jack Green, should I have brought all these solutions to you at the start of the evening? Sure and I would've been spared your black temper if I had."

Jack shook his head. "Other problems would've just jumped in to take their place, and I would've been right back where I started." He looked down at Patrick gratefully. "You taught me how to fish … literally."

Jack looked up to find that the others were leaving their seats and forming a line in the entryway.

"We have one last tradition for new graduates," Patrick explained as he ushered Jack to the hallway, and directed him to stand facing his trainers at the door.

Cordelia came forward, asking Jack if he still had the key ring she'd given him earlier that evening. Jack rummaged in his pocket and pulled out the gold ring with *Every Opportunity Has Its Root in a Relationship* inscribed on its surface.

"All the other relationship keys hang from this principle," she said. "Successful people understand this and try to add people to their city of influence every chance they get." Cordelia hugged him and whispered in his ear, "Good luck, Jack."

Patrick then handed him the first key, which had *Exit the Coliseum* inscribed on its surface. "The first step to building a city of influence is the decision to leave the life of a gladiator behind you."

Patrick urged Jack to put the key on the ring right away. "It's good luck," he explained.

William Bradford waited for Jack to twist the first key onto the ring before stepping forward and handing Jack a gold key which had *Decide to Govern* etched onto it.

"While gladiators attack and defend, governors plant and cultivate," he told him. "As you enter a new world, make sure you do it as a governor and help all those under your leadership to do the same."

Ron came next and placed a surprisingly heavy key in Jack's hand. It read *Recognize That Bricks Trump*, and as Jack twisted it onto the ring, it fell against the other keys with a satisfying clunk.

"If price and performance are equal, the level of relationship will trump. Building with bricks will protect you from all those big bad wolves out there," Ron said. Then in an undertone he added, "You're not still mad about the whole pig thing, are you?"

Jack grinned. "No. Actually, I think you may have been right. It could end up being one of my favorite parts of the training." He punched Ron lightly on the shoulder and added, "But I do plan on returning the favor someday."

Angela came next, placing a key in his hand that read *Avoid Relationship Arrogance.*

"Everyone has hidden influence," she told him. "Never assume you know what people have to offer. Some of your most valuable opportunities will come from the least likely of places."

"Thanks, Angela. I'll be back if any of my symptoms flare up," Jack replied, taking the key with a grateful smile.

Kris's deep laugh rang out as he stepped forward. He put his arm around Jack and handed him the fifth key: *Develop Relationships Just Because.*

"People can sense whether your motives are genuine. Remember to build relationships 'just because' and concentrate on seeing people for who they really are."

For some reason Jack always got emotional around Kris, but he managed to get out a husky, "Thank you."

Chase and Mark came next.

"Pollinate like a bee instead of dining and ditching like a parasite," Chase reminded him, and Mark handed him a key that had *Learn, Serve, Grow* engraved on it.

"Use the Learn, Serve, Grow cycle to build lasting relationships, and don't forget to let others reciprocate. And don't forget we're doing lunch on Friday," Mark added with a grin.

Maggie's key was suspended from a hook, and had *Swim in Pools* etched on its surface. She stepped forward and handed it to Jack.

"Pools are the most effective places to build relationships. Take time to get out of the current and into pools," she said. "And don't be afraid to create a few of your own."

She gave Jack a huge hug and moved on.

Holding a vial of rich amethyst liquid clenched in his fist, Milo approached Jack and handed it to him. It disappeared in a poof of smoke, leaving a gold key in Jack's outstretched hand that had *Measure Influence* engraved on it.

"Only after you have measured your current level of influence can you take the next step of increasing it," he said.

Patrick then held out the last key, *Establish Relationship Laws & Systems*, and handed it to Jack.

"As the governor, 'tis your duty to establish the relationship laws and systems of your organization," he said.

As the final key was added to the ring, the trainers gathered around Jack to congratulate him. Talking and laughing with each other, they gradually drifted out the front door and congregated on the porch that wrapped around the front of the house.

Evening had arrived, and the breeze was drenched with the smell of honeysuckle. Some of the trainers took a seat on the cushioned lawn chairs while others settled themselves on the thick porch railing, swinging their legs as they talked. Patrick and Jack sat down together on either side of the front step, leaning their backs against the finely carved balusters for support.

"Aligning your life and your business with the relationship keys is going to be a difficult challenge, lad," Patrick said slowly. "Sure, isn't that the reason I wanted to bring you here, so you could see for yourself that in the end, the sacrifice would be worth it."

Swallowing a couple of times, Jack absently sifted the gold keys through his fingers.

"How can I ever thank you?" he finally said.

Patrick smiled and put his arm around Jack's shoulders. "I believe you just did, lad. You're a credit to your great-great grandfather, and I've a feeling that you're going to end up just like him. Good night, Jack Green. 'Tis time you finally got some rest."

Jack heard the muffled clanging of a grandfather clock inside the mansion. His eyes grew heavier and heavier, and the porch lights began to fade and blur. The next thing he knew, he felt his right cheek pressed against something smooth and hard. Reluctantly opening his eyes, Jack gazed down at the dark wood grain of his desk. Morning light was streaming through the window, and Jack looked around the room through half-closed eyes, rubbing his face.

"Wow, that was something else," Jack murmured to himself.

As he stood, he felt something jangle in his robe pocket, and emptied out Will Clay's business card, a scrap of paper with the names Mark had given him, and a ring of gold keys.

Looking at the keys, a determined feeling started building inside his chest; he felt infused with gratitude and goodwill. He quickly composed an e-mail inviting his staff to a mandatory meeting the next day, then rummaging through a desk drawer, he found the stack of business cards he'd collected at the Oak Grove Entrepreneur's Group. He shuffled through them until he found David Edwards' card, then picked up the phone and dialed the number.

"David, my name is Jack Green. We met the other day at the Oak Grove Entrepreneur's Group?"

Jack listened into the receiver for a moment.

"That's right," Jack said. "You mentioned you were looking for another round of funding, and I think I know someone that may be able to help. What are you doing for lunch on Tuesday?"

Need help building your city?

If you would like to learn more about the tools and training provided by Corporate Alliance please visit us at:

www.knoweveryone.com

Relationship Keys

Every Opportunity has a root in a relationship.

RELATIONSHIP KEY ONE
Exit the Coliseum

Gladiators make self-preservation their primary
concern and personal victory their
highest ambition.

RELATIONSHIP KEY TWO
Decide to Govern

Mayors make the success of the residents inside their
city of influence their highest priority.

RELATIONSHIP KEY THREE
Recognize That Bricks Trump

When price and performance are equal, the level of
relationship will trump.

RELATIONSHIP KEY FOUR
Avoid Relationship Arrogance

Relationship Arrogance: Prioritizing a relationship
based on a forecasted return on investment.

RELATIONSHIP KEY FIVE
Develop Relationships Just Because

Just Because: The possession of authentic motives.

RELATIONSHIP KEY SIX
Learn, Serve, Grow

The learn, serve, grow cycle: The process of building sustainable relationships.

RELATIONSHIP KEY SEVEN
Swim in Pools

Current: Fast-paced, task-centered environments
Pools: Slow-paced, people-centered environments

RELATIONSHIP KEY EIGHT
Measure Influence

Level 0: Non-resident
Do I have data?

Level 1: Tourist
Have we had at least one positive interaction?

Level 2: Renter
Have we had multiple positive interactions?

Level 3: Homeowner
Do we share an established Learn, Serve, Grow cycle?

Level 4: Developer
Do we give each other access to our time, influence, and resources?

RELATIONSHIP KEY NINE
Establish Relationship Laws and Systems

Sources

Chapter 2: Patrick O'Flannery

Dickens, *Charles*. *A Christmas Carol*. 1st ed. Cambridge, MA: Candlewick Press, 2006. First published December 19, 1843.

Chapter 3: The Gladiator

Source for *Habet, hoc habet:* Literal translation is "He's had it."
http://penelope.uchicago.edu/~grout/encyclopaedia_romana/gladiators/habet.html

Chapter 5: The Governor

Bradford, William. *Of Plymouth Plantation*. New York: Capricorn Books, c1962. First published in 1856 under *History of Plymouth Plantation*.

Chapter 6: Self-Made Myths

Walt Disney

Eliot, Marc. *Walt Disney: Hollywood's Dark Prince*. New York: Birch Lane Press, 1993.

Gabler, Neal. *Walt Disney: The Triumph of the American Imagination*. New York: Random House, 2006.

Sam Walton

Sebenius, James and Ellen Knebel. "Lou Pritchett: Negotiating the P&G Relationship with Wal-Mart." Harvard Business School Case, President and Fellows of Harvard College. 9-907-011 January 16, 2007.

Walton, Sam and John Huey. *Sam Walton: Made in America; My Story*. New York: Doubleday, 1992.

Bill Gates

Boyd, Aaron. *Smart Money: The Story of Bill Gates.* North Carolina: Morgan Reynolds, 1995.

Gatlin, Jonathan. *Bill Gates: The Path to the Future.* New York: Avon Books, 1999.

Wallace, James and Jim Erickson. *Hard Drive: Bill Gates and the Making of the Microsoft Empire.* New Jersey: John Wiley & Sons, 1992.

Phillip Knight

"Carolyn Davidson." *Wikipedia.* 13 April 2007. Wikipedia Foundation. 7 April 2008. http://en.wikipedia.org/wiki/Carolyn_Davidson

Strasser, J.B. and Laurie Becklund. *Swoosh: The Story of Nike and the Men Who Played There.* New York: Harper Collins Publishers, 1993.

Esteé Lauder

"Cosmetics Queen Esteé Lauder Dies." *BBC News.* 25 April 2004. http://news.bbc.co.uk/go/fr/-/1/hi/world/americas/3658375.stm

Lauder, Esteé. *Esteé: A Success Story.* New York: Random House, 1985.

Larry Page and Sergey Brin

Batelle, John. *The Search: How Google and Its Rivals Rewrote the Rules of Business and Transformed Our Culture.* New York: Penguin Group, 2005.

Vise, David A. *The Google Story.* New York: Random House, 2005.

Chapter 8: Relationship Arrogance

The Godfather. Film. Directed by Francis Ford Coppola. Hollywood, CA: Paramount Pictures, 1972.